CISSP

Beginners Guide to Incident Management
Processes

*Cybersecurity and Ethical Hacking to
Information Security Professionals*

Michael Watley

Published By **John Kembrey**

Michael Watley

Cissp: Beginners Guide to Incident Management
Processes (Cybersecurity and Ethical Hacking
to Information Security Professionals)

ISBN   978-1-77485-526-3

No part of this guidebook shall be reproduced in any form without permission in writing from the publisher except in the case of brief quotations embodied in critical articles or reviews.

Legal & Disclaimer

information provided by this guide. This disclaimer applies to any damages or injury caused by the use and application, whether directly or indirectly, of any advice or information presented, whether for breach of contract, tort, negligence, personal injury, criminal intent, or under any other cause of action.

TABLE OF CONTENTS

Introduction

Information security principles and industry's best practices in 8 areas of CISSP including security and training, risk management asset safety, security engineering security for networks and communication Identity and Access Management security testing and assessment security operations and the security of software developers. The book examines the subject in depth.

The book teaches you'll be ready for the theoretical portion that is the common body of know-how (CBK). What exactly is CBK? As you are likely to know the importance of the job as an professional in information security is unparalleled. To meet these critical tasks and mission-critical objectives in the industry you must be able to comprehend the various components of security information that comprise the complete framework that is known as the common body of information. The CBK comprises eight domains as well as pertinent skills, techniques and the best methods. It is then arranged to ensure that the reader acquires the most comprehensive and relevant knowledge after having studied it.

It doesn't matter if you're new to the world of information security this book will provide an step-by-step guide to help you go at your own pace and master each area. The chapters are broken down into smaller pieces of information to help you be able to absorb and remember more. Each chapter is filled with illustrations, examples as well as tips will help you understand how to remember, retain, and recall the material easily. Thus, even for an initial introduction, these books can be an effective guide.

Chapter 1: Learn, Abide By And Promote Professional Ethics

This section we'll examine what ethics mean and the two kinds of ethical conduct you should be aware of and follow as an CISSP practitioner. Then there is the othertype, that is specific to your workplace.

Ethics are the set of moral rules which govern the behavior of a person. It is one of the most crucial aspects or pillars of information security since it is the moral basis to the security plan. Without a moral code there is no way to truly follow the security strategy.

If we take a look at some of the background regarding computer ethics we will discover that it was developed in the 1940s under Norbert Wiener, a MIT professor. It was later delved into his book The Human Use of Human Beings. In this same year first computer crime of the world was committed. There was no law in place to penalize the perpetrator. In 1973 The Association of Computing Machinery (ACM) adopted the ethics code, and Donn Parker was the leader in the development. The idea for the term computer ethics, it was created by a doctor and teacher Walter Maner, as he discovered that ethical decisions can be challenging when computers are added.

In 1978 in 1978, the Rights to Financial Privacy act made it impossible for the government to access bank records. It was adopted by the U.S. Congress adopted it. Some people such as Terrell Bynum Kames Moor Deborah Johnson and others contributed to the ethics through the publication of important guidelines. In 1988 the Computer Matching Act and Privacy Act was enacted from government officials from the U.S. government, and the goal was to stop the ability of debtors to be identified. in 1992, ACM established personal accountability to the act in 24 declarations that are referred to as the ACM Code of ethics and professional Conduct.

Ethics originates from the Greek word called ethos. The meaning is similar to the characteristics (good behavior) of individuals as well as a collective. Moral ethics, in moral philosophy are defined as the following procedure.

Making smart decisions in your life

Respecting rights and responsibilities

- Making moral decisions

- Making a sound judgment between the right and wrong

There are four kinds of ethics. They are:

Ethics applied: Covers topics like the rights of different species and ethical issues during conflicts.

Meta-ethics: Addresses the moral nature of moral judgement

- Normative ethics: Moral judgment.

(ISC)2 Code of Professional Ethics Cannons

(ISC)2 strongly believes that security professionals who have been certified by (ISC)2 must be able to earn and keep the privileges. Therefore that all (ISC)2 accredited professionals have to adhere to the (ISC)2 ethical codes of conduct. Failure to adhere to this code could cause a suspension or cancellation of certification. This means that it is an essential condition for the certificate.

There are four main and obligatory canons that are part of the code. Let's examine them.

Protection: Guard society and the common good. By doing this, you can build trust and confidence in the public. Also, safeguard your infrastructure. This is a crucial measure.

Honesty: You must to behave with integrity. This means that you behave honestly, honestly and in a responsible manner while adhering to lawful frameworks.

Principles: Provide a efficient and punctual service.

Profession: climb the ladder while protecting your profession.

Organizational Code of Ethics

As previously stated the company must have an ethical code and conduct that it can ensure that its employees follow and observing the rules of security for information as well as any other business practices. It also adds empathy to the table. In actual fact they must adhere to the code of ethics, defend it and identify those who do not adhere to it. So the ethics code can be considered as a set of principles. Security professionals your job is to adhere to these rules, educating and inspire others to follow them and to inspire your team as well as the whole organization. Therefore, good behavior is displayed an exemplary moral character of the company to all stakeholders, which includes suppliers, stakeholders as well as third party suppliers and customers. In turn, it encourages customers to rely on the fundamentals and build stronger relations. The entire process is vital for a successful business.

Furthermore, ethically-sound corporate conduct can help gain trust among colleagues during contracts with government and also helps build trust in other areas too. You'll find that many incidents involving security of information happen because of bad ethical conduct. If you adhere to the rules, you will be among those who base their behavior and thinking on an ethical code of conduct.

Ethics, as you can see here, is a requirement for individuals and models. So, the top management and executives bear the primary responsibility of creating the culture that everyone else can easily adopt it without issue. Many employees can come from diverse backgrounds and collaborate to build an organization's culture. Thus, integrating ethics into the environment is not a difficult task if you have a good plan. However, it might not be as easy as following an example. In the field of psychology people are motivated by rewards. Thus, a properly-designed rewarding program will ensure strength and longevity.

Let's examine the main elements of the code ethics.

Values: Moral organization values, such as honesty integrity, fairness, and integrity Humane perspectives

- Principles

Personal responsibility Accountability and responsibility

Support for management - Management support aspects of the ethical regulatory program is its initialization at the top and then flow from top to bottom. The program must be further strengthened with a rewarding program.

Compliance: The code of conduct of ethics could significantly impact and help ensure compliance with standards.

The fundamental steps for creating the code of ethics

Review the current standards and position of ethical conduct through analyzing the interactions of the past and present.

Review the business documents and policies applicable to a variety of areas, such as the onboarding process, use of personal devices, the use of off hours, for example.

- Analyze ethical dilemmas encountered

Implementation

Review process: Each stakeholder and employee must be in the process.

Discuss workplace issues at work (i.e. romantic or relationships, grudges)

Create roles, assign the responsibilities, and make use of role models.

Review the legality with the department of law

- Edit and then publish

Review and monitor

1.6 Create, document and implement Security Policy Standards, Procedures and Security Guidelines

We're moving now from the initialization stage of the security framework/strategies to the phase of implementation. It is recommended to go back and review the earlier sections if you've not completed it in a timely manner.

In the process of developing of distribution, communication, and development (awareness training) this is now the responsibility of the management. The usual procedure is to begin by creating the security framework or use an existing framework as an assistance. The development of security guidelines could be started from this moment. The policy requires the oversight of the head/chairperson/CEO, and they need to approve it. After they have passed it to motion, a board must approve it and review it regularly.

A security policy for information functions as a definition and as a statement of the way an organization can be able to protect and apply security practices and principles (for instance, the way in which proper care are practiced). That is, what the organization intends to do to protect its assets and its values. Take the security policy for the first step towards an organized and well-structured security architecture.

When this has been the initial step, the next is nothing but setting guidelines or standardization. It is possible to think of them as rules or, in the sense of they are rules that must be followed. It will then be developed based on these standards.

In the next phase, there's a need to establish guidelines. What are your thoughts on guidelines? You adhere to the guidelines. What kind of guidance is needed here? In order to implement or create a guidelines, standards or any other type of policy is required, you must have an established set of rules to adhere to. This is the reason for guidelines. A different guideline will also be employed to guide employees, customers, and other others in the security program.

In the end, following guidelines and standards The management team will develop policies and procedures. In the event that we shift back to the guidelines, a policy will not include specific. It just outlines the objectives. Thus, a policy is not a standard or an outline. Because it's not specific, it's not an approach to control. In addition, it is important be aware that a policy doesn't provide the details of implementation or details. It's the job of the procedures. Then, a policy is can be described as it is a definition. It assists in defining the things that need to be secured and how to control it properly through the process of implementation and development. The term "control" is what to safeguard, and what restrictions are set. This is crucial for ensuring the correct selection of products and adhere to the best practices, like.

Standards

The importance of standards is when you are at the point of implementation. Standards define the framework for security and processes. In reality, a standard can assists in decision-making for example, when purchasing equipment such as servers, or software to aid in businesses make decisions, or in the event of purchasing other technologies.

Companies select particular standards (a couple) and then move forward by following it. When an item or procedure is not covered by any specific standards and is not standardized, it could be left without a standard (may be vulnerable or have issues of interoperability). The significance of having a standard is that it guarantees that the standard is used within your specific environment, and that it complies with particulars in the industry, stays within the rules and regulations, and is in compliance.

If we look at a basic example, a policy would require an organization to implement multi-factor authentication. Then, the business chooses to utilize smart cards. They choose a particular standard after consulting with the security analyst, and understanding the policies. Their ultimate goal is interoperability. Interoperability is an attribute of a product or system. It ensures that the system's interfaces are comprehended, and are able to be used with any other product or system in a seamless manner. If they adhere to a standard, they will be able to ensure interoperability as well as security of the entire operation.

Procedures

The procedures directly regulate the process of development. Like we said previously, it is an outline of step-by step instructions regarding how to apply security guidelines. Thus, procedures are required. It is equally important to record these procedures in order to help troubleshoot, reverse engineer and follow when needed and to make any upgrades to. Thus, properly written procedural documents will save you time and money.

These examples illustrate procedures that cover various areas of an company.

- Control of access

- Administrative

Auditing

Configuration

- Security monitoring

- Incident response

Guidelines

Guidelines are guidelines that provide details and guidelines. While they aren't mandatory guidelines, they perform a significant job of transferring information. It is an important method of communicating to raise aware. This is why it is an effective method of distributing information about warnings, rules such as prohibitions, sanctions as well as ethics and thereby bringing aware. For example, a policy could be set up to instruct what a person needs to do in order to adhere to the best methods, i.e., safeguarding passwords.

Baselines

A baseline is in fact a benchmark that is considered to be the ground zero. In the sense of having a minimum security level for CISSP which is required to fulfill a legal requirement. It can be modified to meet business needs, including business policies and compliances, standards and various other aspects. For example the firewall is an initial configuration. A server also has an initial configuration. It's provided to meet minimal requirements that are standard. A baseline will also meet the essential necessities, i.e., protection.

To establish a baseline, you need to develop an official policy. In this instance the form of a security plan. For example, if it's an Windows group policy, which was developed through an initiative for security policies, when it is deemed to be a good fit by the administrator, they will utilize various methods to implement it. After it has been set up, the baseline will be saved or stored for use in the future. These baselines can be used when preparing new systems.

It is important to be aware that an organization typically uses only one baseline per product, or configuration. There are specific instruments to build baselines. Another major function that a base plays is its ability to measure advanced configuration against it. This can be useful for benchmarking.

1.7 Determine, Analyze Prioritize and Identify business continuity (BC) Requirements

Business continuity is the most important priority for any business. Continuity is important when concerns with financial or other matters that impacting your business. But this does not necessarily mean that continuity of business isn't a problem in the absence of any imminent risks, threats or issues that are ongoing. Because, in the event of future risks and threats that are not present today are things you can't be sure not to happen.

In simpler words, business continuity refers to maintaining critical operations in the most dire of scenarios. Business continuity is in tandem and disaster recovery. If there's a chance that is present, it is necessary to plan to ensure business continuity. If the risk is affecting the company, it has to be able to recover from the damage. This is the time when disaster recovery becomes an important factor.

When we discuss business continuity and disaster recovery, we also discuss disaster recovery. Actually, both disaster recovery and business continuity require a comprehensive management approach. If we break down the steps in this way, the team that is accountable for business continuity planning (this typically is led by the top management of the company and managed by the board) establishes a framework that they are able to identify possible dangers. It is then possible to develop resiliency. Once they've identified and documented the potential risks and weaknesses (through analysis) it's possible to react to incidents effectively , while protecting the rights of the stakeholder groups. Their priorities would be the brand's reputation, image, or value.

It is also possible to use this process of disaster recovery (DRP) at the phase of implementation as the business continuity procedure (BCP) is an initial planning stage. Another difference is the fact that DRP is very technical. For instance, we have questions such as what happens should we do if our firewall for web goes down on the border? What can we do to fix it? This is obviously related to the DRP. If it's about BCP We could be asking questions like, what happens should we do if an earthquake strikes our headquarters? The prediction and the response need more planning.

Create and document Scope of Work and plan

During this process the management requests approval from the top of the company by preparing the business case

The head must accept it before taking it to the next step of development

Create the plan in collaboration between technical and business teams.

At this point there is a business continuity policies statement (BCPS) and then an Business Impact Analysis (BIA).

Once the process is beyond this point then the next process is developed.

Disaster recovery and business continuity need planning. Thus, the process of planning includes the following key steps.

1. Planning of projects.

2. Business Impact Analysis (BIA).

3. Recovery strategy Formulation.

4. The process is planned, designed and developing.

5. Implementation.

6. Testing and reviewing.

7. Monitoring and maintenance.

When we take in both the BCP and DRP We can see the elements that comprise the whole-of-life approach discussed earlier. There are two components.

1. Business Continuity Process. This includes,

a. Strategies and policies.

b. Risk management.

c. Planning.

2. Verification of implementation.

a. The process of recovering Information Technology.

b. Alternatives (i.e. websites, websites).

C. Maintaining offsite and onsite backups. Replication is another crucial aspect.

Notice: There are a variety of backup websites that you have to be aware of. These include,

Hot site: This kind of site is always up and running. It is possible to configure it in a branch office , often. It can also be set up in a cloud or data center. It should be accessible immediately in the event of a disaster. Furthermore, it should be located away from the main location.

Warm site Warm site: This is a less expensive alternative to a host site but is not able to provide an immediate recovery after an incident. Although this may be true however, it also contains the power, network, servers phones, as well as other resources.

Cold site The cheapest alternative and requires more time to complete a recovery.

Business Impact Analysis (BIA)

Business Continuity Planning Process

While planning is a lengthy and long-winded process, the main steps are easy to comprehend.

1. Finding compliance requirements that could be a problem.

2. Documentation of the requirements that have been identified.

3. Document and identify possible risks, threats and weaknesses.

4. BIA process.

5. Prioritize resources like processes, systems, or units according to the importance of the resource in question.

6. Then, you must determine the procedures for resumption.

7. Transfer the responsibility and tasks.

8. Create guidelines and procedures.

9. Make people aware through training programmes.

10. Examine the procedure.

Methods to Perform an BIA

BIA is a complicated procedure, and knowing the basics can help you in real-world situations. We'll go over some basic terms first.

Maximum Tolerable Downtime, also known as MTD What is the maximum time a business can endure without a damaged component, lost function or even a significant loss? The maximum time is called the MTD.

Recovery Point Objective (RPO) What is the maximum distance you can return and recuperate from? What is the maximum amount that can be repaired? It is called the RPO.

The goal of recovery time is The amount of time needed to recuperate from the loss.

In this light we can now examine the step-by step BIA procedure.

1. Choose the sources of data (i.e. people, organizations) to collect data. Methods such as questionnaires could be utilized in this phase.

2. Employ quantitative and qualitative methods and methods for collecting data.

3. Recognize the essential business processes.

4. Find the objects that are dependent of these functions. Identify the dependent objects on those.

5. Determine the value of MTDs.

6. Find vulnerabilities and threats that could be a threat.

7. Examine the risk and do the necessary calculations in order to define and explain the results.

8. Document all results and prepare the final report.

9. Send the report to management.

In parallel, you can run the steps below.

1. Conduct tests and check the accuracy of the gathered information.

2. Find out the time for recovery.

3. If you are unable to recover, decide on the best option.

4. Estimated the possible costs.

Once you've completed the BIA procedure, you are able to proceed with the process of business continuity as described below.

1. Create a recovery plan and the procedures.

2. Plan development.

3. Reviews and tests (i.e. exercises).

Example Scenario Real-world illustration of the BIA procedure.

1. Create a questionnaire that are similar to the ones mentioned earlier.

2. The person in charge of the BIA should be trained about how you conduct and finish an BIA. You can instruct the person via workshops or by any other method.

3. Take the BIA forms.

4. Perform a review.

5. In the last stage Validate data with interview and follow-ups.

Once you have completed this when you're done, you're ready to go to the next step.

Recovery Strategy

In the next phase, the process of planning and implementation of the recovery process will take place.

1. Since the BIA is completed now is the time to determine and document the needs for resources.

2. Conduct the gap analysis. This will reveal the gaps in current capabilities and the requirements for recovery.

3. The next step is to examine and follow the plan, and then get approval of the management.

4. Implementation and finalization.

Plan Development

In this stage it is the time to carry out the next tasks carried out.

1. The framework is being developed.

2. The formation of teams and the assignment of the roles and the responsibilities.

3. Planning for a relocation.

4. The compilation of disaster recovery and business continuity procedures.

5. Documenting the procedure.

6. The plan must be validated.

7. The process of obtaining the approval of management.

Tests and Evaluations

The most crucial element of this whole procedure is to create an effective strategy for combat. This is, therefore, the most crucial phase of all. This includes,

1. The determination of test requirements or maintenance specifications.

2. Develop testing strategies and exercises.

3. Provide training continuously.

4. Conduct orientation exercises.

5. Conduct the tests and then document the results in a thorough report.

6. Based on lessons learned, you can revise and revise the business continuity plan procedure, process and everything else.

The information in this article you've discovered how to develop a an effective business continuity and disaster recovery strategies. Reviewing and revising the plan are crucial actions. Furthermore, regular checks up of the measures and conducting exercises for training are essential to the success of rehabilitation and mitigation.

Chapter 2: Participate To And Enforce Security Policies For Personnel And Procedures

People are by far the weakest person in a security program. They are able to pose significant and real dangers by either not knowing or being negligent. Anyone using the system could cause severe destruction to the assets and the information. There are intelligent attacks such as phishing and social engineering. There are also more sophisticated attacks such as remote control, viruses ransomware, remote control, and various other types of disclosures. There can also be fake identities. In some cases, due to personal or personal issues there are internal threats, such as man-in the-middle attacks, information leaks or theft, as well as terrorist activity. To mitigate these risks the security policy should be formulated, the procedures documented and in place.

Screening for candidates in the hiring process

This is among the most essential aspects when hiring an employee in addition to other aspects. Candidates must go through various background checks like identities checks, clean record checks against criminal acts (criminal records) as well as recommendations and social media interactions. Additionally, he needs to be confirmed against his previous activities and education, as well as certifications as well as past work and performance as well as medical information, any other information that is required. Additionally, a person may be checked for background by external referees. In these instances, the employer needs to verify who the person who refers to them will be (identity) and also if they are related to the applicant. If the candidate passes with a clean report then it's possible to place him in probation for a period of time.

Employer Agreements, Policies and Employment Contracts

The employee agreement is among the most crucial documents that are used in how to hire. The majority of employers, as and candidates aren't handling this procedure properly. After hiring a candidate they sign an agreement, or agreement with an organization. After signing it and agrees to safeguard it at work and even when away from work, however, when employing corporate assets.

A contract defines the roles of employees obligations, duties, and responsibilities including accountability, wages and onboarding, termination, punishments, and rewards. Sections on accountability, code of conduct are in place with a clause that states employees agree to the penalties and consequences in case the employee fails to follow the.

The agreement should include a clear explanation of the steps the company takes in the event of a problem. This will reduce the chance of frustrations and can justify the systemic method. It should also include how the clearance and termination will be handled to ensure that the employee does not feel a sense of negativity in the process of termination and also how the company will be able to return its assets.

The Onboarding and Termination Process

The process of onboarding begins from the initial contact of the applicant, and continues following the hiring process, until the employee is established within the company. This is essential for everyone in the team, but most importantly for the employee's psychological well-being and technically. It also assists the rookie to become familiar with the organization's culture, to become acquainted with the roles and responsibilities through orientation to the job, become acquainted with the company's and security procedures and make friends to one another.

It also minimized the risks that a new employee could bring to the table or behave without intention. If the procedure is clear simple, easy to understand and understand (makes sense) and well-organized, an employee can feel a part of the team and will be psychologically committed to preserving the rules of conduct, being accountable and accountable and secure (this is among the most difficult, yet crucial objectives).

The process of termination is one which every employee has to undergo at least once in their life time. It's not an easy task for management either. There are general reasons for terminations, such as due to willful leave as well as the expiration of a contract term or exceeding the age limit or age limit, and other such things. There are other difficult situations, such as the termination of an employee because of reduction in costs, the result of seizures of operations, because of the actions of an employee, or simply because of better alternatives. These scenarios are extremely sensitive and require careful planning.

To simplify and speed up the process there should be clear policies and procedures that are well-documented.

The following is an overview of the required screening tasks.

- Screening for pre-employment

Screening for criminal activity

Screening for a sex crime

- Screening for drugs

Tracking Social Security Number

- Credit history

- Compensation claim history

End of Process in short

Record and collect the information

- Request the resignation form (or accept it)

- Notifying the Human Resource department.

Notify the administrators of the system.

- Termination of accounts both digital and non-digital

- Asset revoking checklist

- Dismantle the assets of the company and make a note of the list of items

- Deleting access to the assets, and make sure you have the checklist

- Verify the assets received

- Request a benefit status letter from HR. Once HR has it, you will receive it.

Re-read any agreement that has been signed.

- Make the final payment including any additional payments

If needed, conduct an exit interview and request written permission for references

- - Update your information

- Stop the profile

- Farewell party

Vendor, Consultant and Contractor Contracts and Controls

A vendor may be a manufacturer, supplier, manufacturer, or another similar type of entity. A consultant is typically an outsider offering external services like consulting, auditing the work of contract, as well as guidance. A contractor is a person who will perform an enterprise task or several assignments for an organization for an extended period of duration. For instance, a worker on contract will be employed for a period of two years within an organization. He or she must know when to begin and end the work as per a written agreement.

The potential risk is that, when you allow your company to the outside world it also opens up the possibility of allowing them to operate in full or as part within your business. So, the selection of vendors, their reputation, and the compliance to which they are closely examined and appropriate safeguards and limitations must be in place.

The majority of the time that an organization hires an expert, the consultant will be provided with a dedicated computer as well as connectivity for internal system and information. This comes with particular limitations, obviously. Consultants work with multiple companies. So, they must keep their records in order and have proper monitoring. Also, you should consider the possibility of making mistakes, and the risk of data loss due to accident and corruption MitM attacks, as well as information theft.

This is also the case of vendors. A screening and a compliance check must be carried out. If any specific applications developed by a particular vendor or other components available they must be thoroughly tested. With the help of agreements can be used to mark the boundaries and boundaries.

Compliance Policy Requirements

You are already well-informed about compliance and how to incorporate them into your corporate procedures. In this scenario, employees must be informed and trained as well as assessed to confirm their understanding and conformity to the policies of compliance. There must be a self-guided knowledge base and workshops, seminars and other training events. This way there are a lot of risks diminished through awareness and knowledge.

Privacy Policy Requirements for Privacy

You have already been introduced to entities like Personal Identifiable Information or PII in a previous article. A company is responsible for both internal as well as outside PI Information. This means that the information has to be guarded with utmost care against internal and external threats. To protect such data, the lowest privilege and need to know rules are useful tools.

Any person or process that has access PII should be monitored and scrutinized. In this way the confidence in the institution can be determined.

Furthermore, these regulations and policies should be clearly documented and made clear. The document must describe the kind of information is in danger and what information is protected and how it is addressed.

1.9 Know and apply the Risk Management Concepts

Risk management is the method of identifying, assessing, and responding to risks of determining, assessing and addressing the risks. The risks could be present or future risks. These risks arise from the occurrence of vulnerabilities and threats. There could be additional risks and risks. The process of risk management includes protection and reduction. In order to do this an established and tested plan is essential.

Recognize Threats and Security Risks

If you can recall the information you've learned up to now then you know the definitions you need in your head. A vulnerability can be exploited as a vulnerability. When there's a vulnerability there is a level of possibility that a security threat could emerge to exploit the vulnerability. There could be a variety of vulnerabilities. Some are simple to identify, but others are not obvious. Subject matter experts may discover the vulnerabilities and report them to the responsible individuals. Others may discover an exploit and gain by exploiting it. They are known as threat actors.

How do you control the risks? They are the methods or techniques employed to minimize or limit the vulnerability of the present or in the future. You have already learned about the controls. They are detective, preventive, deterrent, and corrective controls.

Risk Assessment/Analysis

Assessment of the risks

Assessment of risk is the very first step in managing risk. It is crucial to determine the weaknesses and how they could become threats. If a threat agent is able to exploit the vulnerability, there will be an impact of some size. The impact has to be determined in the risk assessment process.

There are several methods to evaluate risks. These include,

Qualitative risk assessment in a qualitative analysis of an event, or regulation is studied. Through studying, we gain an understanding of the level of effectiveness of its application. What is important to know in this case is that a decision was taken regarding the effect on the company when the control isn't implemented. The likelihood of necessity of control of the user is also understood. This can provide the risk assessor data on the extent (the level) that control has been in place currently. This is where an assessment scale could be used. By using these strategies that assess risk, it's possible to determine the risk the risk based on a particular guideline or standard.

Quantitative risk assessment In this approach, the reliable and available data is used to create a the numerical value. Then, it is used to determine the likelihood of the risk.

The hybrid (qualitative as well as qualitative and) Risk assessment method is a hybrid of quantitative and qualitative methods.

Conducting an Quantitative Assessment

As you may have guessed this test is about numbers. That is, figures, and dollar amounts. Costs can be allocated to various elements that are analyzed for risk, as well as to the threats identified, and to assets. The following components are included in this procedure.

- Asset value

Impact

- The frequency of threats

Effectiveness of the safeguards

Costs of safeguards

Probability

Uncertainty

The issue of using this technique is you are unable to accurately determine or assign cost-values to specific components. In these instances the qualitative approach is employed. Let's now look at the method of quantitative assessment.

1. Estimating the risk of loss This is how it is the single loss expectation (SLE) can be calculated. The formula is SLE + Asset Value + Exposure Factor. In this case, the things to take into consideration are the theft of assets destruction of information, physical destruction and loss of data and threats that could delay processing. The exposure is the amount of damage that a threat may cause.

2. Annual Rate of Recurrence (ARO) The ARO answer the question "how many times can you expect to occur per certain duration?"

3. Annual Loss of Expectancy (ALE) The final step is to determine the extent of risk. It is calculated by multiplying ALE x SLE = ARO.

Be sure to record all associated costs like repair costs or replacement and reloading, as well as the value of the equipment or the lost data, as well as the loss of productivity.

Doing the Qualitative Assessment

In this way it is not a case where numbers or dollars are used. Instead, it relies on the scenario. It is not easy or even impossible to assign value to specific assets. Thus, an exact quantitative assessment is not possible. However an absolute qualitative analysis is feasible.

There is the possibility to classify the losses according to the scale, such as that of low, medium or high. A risk of low can be considered to be a minor or short-term loss, and moderate risk can cause moderate damage to an organization and may include repairs. Risks that are high can lead to devastating losses, such as the loss of reputation, legal actions that are followed by a fine or even a loss of a substantial amount of revenues.

The problem with this method is that you are unable to effectively explain the principles.

There are several methods to conduct qualitative assessments, including FRAP (Facilitated Risk Assessment Process) and Delphi.

Risk Response

To deal with the threat, it is necessary to have a methodical approach. There are four main steps that are possible to take. They are

Risk mitigation: Risks cannot be avoided all the time. Making the effort as minimal as possible is the most effective method.

Risk assignment or placement or placing risk refers to transferring or assigning the expense of the loss that risk entails to another entity. It could be a different organization such as a vendor or an equivalent entity. Examples include outsourcing and insurance.

Acceptance of risk Risk acceptance: This is the standard process of taking on the risk.

Risk rejection The risk rejection act of not recognizing that there is no risk. It can result in dangerous consequences, however, some organizations would prefer this route.

Countermeasures Selection and implementation

Implementation and implementation of countermeasures, controls or security measures is an essential measure to reduce risk. They can be physical (humans or hardware, fences or dogs) or more logical (software like firewalls) or even hybrid (hardware firewalls, along with other functions of software).

If we look at a straightforward example of security for passwords it is possible to block reversible encryption of passwords by using names and commonly used words. You can also increase the strength with a greater number of characters as well as the characters required. Additionally you can set up two-factor or multi-factor authentication.

There are a variety of countermeasures available for every component, point and the perimeter. The choice should be made following an appropriate evaluation process, and the team needs to be able to install, configure and manage the security measures and controls.

Controls that are applicable to certain types of controls

There are various kinds of controls. You were familiar with the controls earlier. They are

- Controls to prevent

- Detective controls

- Corrective controls

- Deterrent controls

Recovery controls: These are designed to help with recovery. There could be numerous scenarios of general data loss, hardware failure corruption, data theft or physical damage, as well as other catastrophes. The best way to prevent this is through processes for recovery and backup networks-attached disks Storage Area Networks, Clustering disk arrays (RAID kinds) and software.

- Compensation controls

Security Control Assessment (SCA)

A security audit is one of the most important elements of the security plan. It is important because if you do not periodically assess it, you are unable to detect flaws, required changes - updates/upgrades/retirements/obsoletions, vulnerabilities, and budgetary concerns.

Certain tools can be used to perform an SCA. For example, NIST SCA aids in conducting a thorough SCA. For more information refer NIST Special Publication 800-53 Monitoring and Measuring

Monitoring is the most important aspect of an effective security program. It is crucial to monitor the deployment and implementation, and then optimize it to achieve the best performance and accuracy. This will ensure sustainability since it can help to reduce the risk of unknown and future threats constantly. This procedure must be defined and followed by an appropriate team.

Let's consider an example to see why it's important. You have set up the perimeter firewall and believe all will be in order. In the end, your firewall is exposed to various kinds of scans and records the scans. But, you're not paying attention to the scans, and you don't create a proper alerting process. At the end of the day, following an extended period of investigation and investigation, an attacker uncovers an exploit, and launches an attack and is successful. penetrates the boundary.

As you can see it appears that you weren't aware of the vulnerability since you believed that this was only a one-time configuration. You didn't patch or make the necessary updates to the firewall. Furthermore, you have not create an alerting program, and you forgot to establish an alerting system that alerts those responsible for an incident. Additionally, you might not have put in place an emergency backup and recovery procedure when someone violates. The failures of all these points at a common flaw, security procedures.

Thus, a reliable monitoring system with alerts appropriate thresholds, correctly configured thresholds automated locking down functions and a prompt update/patching program are required for these types of situations. Another crucial step is to protect the logs. If you are looking to find any events, you must have the logs. So, backing up and securing up logs is a crucial step particularly when log rotation occurs. periodic reviews and auditing of the logs will assist to discover the causes of the incident as well as future threats and weaknesses. It is crucial to maintain contacts with your vendor and their information in order to be able to timely make updates and patches to the assets.

In an overall organizational setting the reviewing and monitoring processes are performed every week. During the review process it is expected that the following areas will be emphasized.

Number of instances

Nature of the happenings that result in both success and the failure

Duration

- Assets affected

Impact

Locations and involved parties

Valuation of Assets

The value of assets plays a significant function in the process of risk management. In every organization the management needs to be aware of the different types of property, including intangible as well as tangible, and their values. There are a variety of methods used for valuing assets.

Cost method It is calculated based on the initial cost of the asset at the time it was first purchased.

Market value method This method is based on the price of an asset when it is sold on the market. If the asset isn't readily available on the market There are two other ways to go about it. These are:

* Value of replacement In the event that an asset similar to this is available for purchase using that information the value is determined.

* Net realizable values: The sale value of an asset (if it is able to be sold) and subtracted by the cost.

The average cost method: The total cost of the goods offered for sale divided by units that are available. If the value cannot be determined from the available units, this is an appropriate option to apply.

Base-stock method: Each business has a set amount of stock. Therefore, it is dependent on the worth of this base-stock.

Reporting

Alerts and reports play an important part in the process, and this has been repeatedly stressed. They aid in determining the needs and requirements. This allows the organization to effectively utilize the resources and countermeasures. It also helps in the and proactive handling of security concerns and protects the organization's assets, including the information.

When preparing a report, it's crucial to remember that the report needs to reflect the risk-taking capabilities of the company. When you write a report, you should follow a certain. It needs to be clarified your thoughts, and at times, you can't make your report too complex. The report needs to be understood or, more precisely for all participants. Also, you should take into consideration the rules set forth by the current laws, directives regulations, or other regulations or standards are in place within your company.

Continuously Improve

This emphasizes the need for constant improvement to ensure that the risk management and recovery plan up-to-date and free of errors. Also, this is an incremental process and is able to apply it at any level and function within an organisation.

To assist in this process, make use of to aid in this process, you can use the ISO/IEC 27000 family. It specifies the guidelines for a complete Information Security Management System (ISMS) in the following clauses: 5.1, 5.2, 6.1, 6.2, 9.1, 9.3, 10.1, and 10.2.

Risk Frameworks

It is important to have assistance in developing a proper and precise risks assessment and resolution and monitoring strategies so that the result is a sound risk management procedure. That's why you have to implement an appropriate risk framework. There are a variety of risk frameworks that have been created and readily available. The most renowned and well-known risk frameworks include,

- NIST Risk Assessment Framework:

- Operationally Critical Threat, Asset, and Vulnerability Evaluation (OCTAVE): versions 2.0 for enterprises as well as the version OCTAVE-S v1.0 for medium and small enterprises.

Chapter 3: Learn And Apply The Concepts And Methods Of Threat Modeling

It is a strategy used to quantify and identify dangers so that the threat are communicated and prioritized. This technique is widely used in the process of developing software.

Techniques to model threats are focused upon one or more of these areas.

- Attacker

Asset

Software

Some of the well-known and well-known threat modeling techniques are as follows.

Method to simulate attacks and Threat Analysis (PASTA) is a risk-based modeling technique.

Stomping on Identity, Tampering Refusal, Disclosure and denial of Service, Elevation of Privilege (STRIDE) created as a security measure by Microsoft. For more information, visit Visual, Agile and Simplified Threat (VAST) VAST is a different threat modeling framework that is based on the platform ThreatModeler.

You can also employ CVSS, OCTAVE, NIST, LINDDUN and numerous others. The selection of the tool depends on the requirements, accessibility, and the particular scenario.

Alongside these techniques and tools using them, you may also use other tools, like threats rating and rating. These are used to evaluate and assign amount of weight to each threat, so that it can be utilized in modeling to gain a better understanding of. Damage Reproducibility, Exploitability Affected Users and Findability (DREAD) from Microsoft is an illustration. As you might be aware, it can be used for risk analysis using a qualitative analysis. Remember this aggregated model an excellent model.

Let's look at the steps of threat modeling to help us understand.

1. Identification phase

2. Decribing the architecture

3. Dissolving the process

4. Threats classified

5. Categorizing threats

6. Assessing the dangers

1.11 Apply risk-based management concepts in the Supply Chain

When we have developed a complete risk management strategy It is then possible to use it in a variety of aspects of business and functions. In this case it's utilized in areas of supply management. The company might have to deal with external entities including contractors, suppliers transportation and logistics providers as well as many other. To reduce risk and recuperate from any kind of disruption, you need to apply the concepts of risk-based management in this field since it is a risky area such as outages and threats. Similar concepts applies to mergers and acquisitions. If you've followed up to this point, you must have realized that this is an instance in which due diligence is required.

The risk associated with hardware Software, Services, and Hardware

This section we'll be looking at the risk of these assets in addition to live-ware and humans. Every new and old hardware software, hardware, and even services increase the risk profile of an enterprise. If they are not adequately managed and determined by a risk framework these elements pose a significant risk to the viability of the company. Additionally, it could cause integration and interoperability issues and compliance issues.

When buying new hardware there are a lot of factors to be considered so you are able to ensure security and safety. The vendor must be able to provide continuous support for maintenance of the hardware by providing patches as well as updates and guidance regarding security. When it comes to integration you must take into account the risk it poses.

Software On the other hand presents more risk because, unlike a device it carries software and security layers problems. There could be issues at the level of the component, the modular levels, the compilation stage and other levels. A few architectural features could create problems. Furthermore, when you are using different features such as this, it could bring risk, particularly revealing internal data like IP addresses to remote servers as well as customer data particularly if you are using cloud-based software. These can pose even greater risks to cyber-based risks. In addition, compliance requirements can have restrictions on these choices.

The services are the more complex matrix. The term "service" could refer to greater human involvement in addition to software-based services. For instance, an online service provider offers a variety of internet-based services to a variety of companies. This is why it's the primary information route for all outside activities , as well as for clients who depend on services offered by the company. Even though ISPs offer assurances of service and safety, services that an company provides are not provided outside of the organization, and the resources that are used to connect to the internet, must be secured from threats to the internet, such as trojan horses scams including phishing, sniffing, and other types of attacks including DDoS.

Evaluation and monitoring by a Third Party

It is impossible for any organization to live without the help of third parties, because they are a part of the supply chain. only a single entity is able to sustain. In addition to the many other aspects, to protect assets within the organization and information shared with others Non-disclosure agreements, privacy and security agreements as well as any service level agreements (SLAs) should undergo a review by both the business's director and board of directors. Following the review process it is possible to compare the goals of the organization the security architecture, compliant requests and standards are assessed.

Minimum Security Requirements

Each component that comes initially enters the business of the company must meet a set of security requirements that are minimum. This acts as a base. On this basis, necessary security measures can be developed and be shared with other individuals. It also aids to close security holes, allowing to assess new requirements, identify and resolve weaknesses, and then implement the appropriate security measures.

After the security requirements have been determined, they should be continuously reviewed at a minimum at the level of functional. A complete annual review is also necessary. Furthermore, after the acquisition or merger it is necessary to manage change. The need for a transition period is essential in this case. During this transition time the security policies, procedures , practices, compliance requirements and regulations must be taken into consideration.

Service-Level Agreement Requirements

An agreement to provide service or an SLA is mostly a measurement of excellence in service in terms of performance and quality. It is often used in conjunction with performance indicators and important performance indicators (KPI). In the case of an organization, delivering services to clients in time or within a reasonable timeframe is crucial. So, most organizations which offer services have SLAs in place, and when they offer services, customers and the service provider agree to the terms.

A company, for instance, might offer a cloud-based service for its customers. They must offer one or more SLAs according to the level of subscription. Here's an example.

Responding to urgent tickets or calls with 15 minutes or less for subscribers who are premium. This is done by the account administrator.

Responding to urgent tickets within one hour. Support via chat for those customers.

Responding to issues that are not critical in 24 hours. This is usually done through tickets.

An organization could have agreements with those they rely on, for example the Internet service supplier or cloud provider. When purchasing these services, an organization should review the SLAs and performance records. SLA provides quality service, in terms of speedy reaction and restoration. For services that are mission-critical, these dependencies could cause serious harm for businesses in the event that these third-party or external providers are not able to meet the SLAs. There are risks and the business must be aware of them as far as it is possible.

There are also other agreements, like the following.

Operating Level Agreements (OLA) Operating Level Agreements (OLA) serve as internal level agreement for service that are designed to be used by internal users. OLAs are comprised of service tags, similar to SLAs and can be used to measure internal performance.

underpinning contracts (UC) It measures the performance of a service provider (external) and the supplier of services (external).

Service management is an integral part of any organization, particularly in the case of organizations that provide any kind of service. If you've taken a course in ITSM or ITIL You are exposed to the OLAs as well as SLAs in detail. OLAs typically comprise of,

- Service desk

Support groups

- Administration of systems

- Management of operations

- Incident management

The fundamental model of an SLA comprises,

A master service contract Also referred to the MSA

-- SLA and KPI

- - One or more OLAs

Chapter 4: Create And Maintain The Security Awareness, Education And Training Program

In every company the weakest link in any organization isn't a gadget or software, but the users and employees. Thus, a well-organized training program designed by the chief of the company is a crucial success aspect. Insufficient awareness and lack of technical knowledge can lead employees to make errors and cause discontent, anger and inattention. Controlling this is an additional crucial element that is part of managing risk.

Techniques and Methods to Create Awareness and to Train

The most vital aspect of a training initiative is to create an assumption about this. Most of the time, leaders of an organization don't trust in a properly designed training program. They undervalue their capabilities and don't care whether employees don't possess the right knowledge. Instead, they trust other teams, like IT administration IT administrators, who create all arrangements. This is the reason why the program will likely be a failure.

The first step is to have the appropriate skill professionals together with or without consultants, write and draft the security plan. The management and board accountable for the program must be aware of the programand have to demonstrate the required qualifications and skills through education and the granting of certification.

The next step is to raise aware and communicating the pertinent information to other managers and departments in particular non-technical employees. It is a top-level training program that is focused on the process of orienting. Once they have this accomplished then they can increase their skills and share the skills, knowledge and techniques to their team members. Here are a few steps to manage this program thoroughly.

1. The head of the company and the management at the top meet and discuss what they need to provide and convey to the lower management levels.

2. The training plan is created by the top management, who actively participates in the whole training program.

3. The presentation offers clear views and the ways it can benefit businesses in the near and long-term.

4. The demonstrations should be able to explain the benefits to sustainability and how it can benefit employees in a clear and concise manner.

5. The goal of the program should be the development of a foundation.

6. To make it more interesting and engaging, presentation techniques such as stories, graphics, appealing multimedia, visuals and digital environments like remote capabilities and conferencing tools are a great way to reduce space and time.

7. The program of training should be fun and enjoyable.

8. During the course there must be an assessment of the level of awareness and understanding.

9. Regular workouts (without telling them) could expose the truth.

10. Keep updating the program and the content.

11. Regular training.

12. Assessment and learning center set up for those who wish to learn more about the subject and obtain certifications.

Another aspect that is crucial to training is the capability to make use of colleagues as well as vendors, consultants and institutes, such as, (ISC)2.

Periodic Content Reviews

The training content and materials is required to be regularly updated as technologies evolve, and replaced or updated, security issues and the content is constantly updated. New security vulnerabilities and threats may emerge.

Also, the content needs to be easy to comprehend for non-technical users. As we mentioned before the content needs to be interactive and practical. Additionally, it is possible to conduct these kinds of workshops, training programs or webinars via social media networks. Tools for collaboration like Microsoft Office 365 brings new levels of training.

Evaluation of Program Effectiveness

To determine the efficacy for the programme, it needs to be a criterion for evaluation. For instance, it's possible to use performance indicators. Following training and then after your training session, you could set up periodic testing to ensure that employees will be tested on their degree of their awareness. As an example, you may try to trick users with various methods If the results are lower than those of previous tests, it is a positive improvement.

Chapter 5: Domain 2 Asset Security Asset Security

The definition of an asset is: A asset is an item that is considered to be its the owner of an organisation. Additionally, it has a importance to the business. An asset could be the person, a bit of data or information or a structure, device, or even a deed. We've already discussed asset in our previous chapters. This chapter is focused on protecting the assets. In reality, it's concerned with safeguarding information or data as they are the most important assets. Information security is the principal element of a successful security strategy and is the duty of an CISSP qualified professional.

Before we get into the security techniques it is best to understand what data is. Data is the basic unit of information, which includes bits and bits of knowledge scattered. Data has different states. It may be in stationary, in motion, transformed, or being utilized. Wen together, data can provide meaningful information.

Also, data has a lifecycle. It is created and stored, then used as well as transformed, archived and then deleted. Through the entire process the organization has to protect the information using CIA procedures and following the security plan. But, data may be different in the context of an company. Certain data may be crucially vital, while other data may be sensitive to specific departments or roles, while certain data may be helpful. It is important to identify the importance and importance when it comes to protecting data. To accomplish this, we apply the method of classification of data.

2.1 Identify and classify information and Sssets

Classification of Data

Data needs to be identified, classified and then tagged to ensure that the information and data are open to a certain person. To recognize the data that is categorised you must perform the tagging. It is called Labeling.

Another goal of classification of data is to assign the responsibility for data to specific roles. Others roles are not able to access the information unless the guardian gives the key. This is known as clearing. Only the individual who had the intention to gain access to the data will be the sole one to have access.

If someone is in need of access to their data, they will need undergo an approval procedure for access. To secure the security of data, we employ two rules. One of them is the need-to-know. This means that the knowledge of the user is limited to what the user must know but not more than the limit. The second is known as the person with the lowest privilege. This means that the person has the lowest authorization to do any kind of work with the data.

If an individual needs access to data not his the data owner, they must have access granted. Once granted permission, the user has to be informed of the sensitivity of the data, as well as how they should safeguard it as well as the restrictions that are placed upon the information. To keep track of and audit the actions of users and how they do it, they need to undergo the authorization, authentication, and auditing procedures. This is also referred to by the acronym triple-A (AAA). To grant the access needed to do a job that requires the least privilege to be granted.

A number of countries follow legislation from the government and implement the classification process. For instance, in the U.S., the executive order 12356 applies to national security data. After classifying, declassifying and protecting information, this order can be used. In various countries, there are various methods.

Data Considerations for Classification

Data security

Access rights

- Data encryption

- Data retention

- Data disposal

Use of data,

Regulations and conformity requirements.

Labeling

Let's take a look at the various kinds of labeling.

Top Secret The highest security level that is applied to military and government information. The disclosure of such information could cause great harm to the nation.

Hidden: The following class. An organization's leak of information of this kind can cause huge destruction and damage to reputation.

If the information is disclosed the information could cause damage the amount for an organisation or nation.

Sensitive but Not Classified This information can impact individuals in the event that it's released. For example, a person's medical condition could cause personal loss and social problems.

For Use in Office Only

Unclassified

Asset Classification

This section's emphasis will be on the data asset as well as physical assets. Asset classification is also utilized in security of information, but it is more commonly used in accounting.

2.2 Find and Keep the Asset Ownership and Information

The owner of the data is the person assigned to oversee, maintain and protect the asset. This is also the case for data. To ensure the security of data, it must have an owner. The person who owns the data is accountable and accountable for the actions that happen to the data. Data owners must also be involved in the classification of data, implementing guidelines and rules, authorization as well as authorization. Clearance secure, retain and destruction of all devices and data.

2.3 Secure Privacy

To protect security, data is allocated to and maintained by a variety of roles. It is important to be familiar with the roles as well as how they handle information.

- Mission Owners: Have the responsibility to create the process of establishing, funding, and implementing the proper security plan to protect information.

- Data owner The majority of data owners are data managers. They are accountable for data classification retention, labeling, backup/recovery, as well as disposal are the most crucial.

- Custodian of data: This is someone who has been delegated duties. For example, a database owner could appoint a custodian to back up data in accordance with a scheduled. Certain system-level custodians manage the system by applying updates and patches.

Systems Owners: Just as the title implies, this job is accountable for the management and maintenance of systems that house information. Network administrators, server managers, and system administrators take on the role in a variety of ways.

Users: Individuals who modify and use data. However, this does not mean that they're not responsible. In fact, they are the ones with the greatest responsibility as they can expose, corrupt or erase information. In this instance they are required to adhere to the guidelines by undergoing instruction.

Control and Processors of Data Controllers and Processors of Data

An individual who is a Data Controller as per to European Commission, is the one who "determines the purpose of the data processing and the methods for how personal data are processed. If your company or organization decides "why" and "how the personal data will be processed, it's that data controller. Personal data processing employees within your company do this in order to fulfill the duties of the controller of data."

The Data processor On the other hand is responsible for managing all data for the controller. The definition given by the European Union says, "The data processor handles personal data exclusively for the control. The processor of data is typically an external third-party to the business. In the event of groups of companies the same undertaking can be an intermediary for another."

A data controller is an data processor when it comes to an entirely different set of data. This is the reason for the "However when it comes to the situation of groups of companies an undertaking could serve as processor for another."

A joint controller of data as per the EU's definition, is "Your business or organization is a joint controller when, along and with other other organizations, it determines in concert what the reason for and how personal data is to be handled. Joint controllers have to sign an agreement outlining their respective responsibilities in order to be compliant with GDPR regulations. The principal elements of the agreement must be disclosed to the people who are processing the data."

Data Remanence

Data storage could represent a serious security risk as conventional methods might not completely eliminate the data once deleted. This is the case for magnetic disks as well as magnetic tapes. Thanks to the advancements in technology there are methods to retrieve data using the latest storage technologies. Data remanence may lead to exposure of data. The technology variety (RAM, Flash, ROM, SSD, etc.) makes the threat more severe.

The destruction of data

You are aware of the risk to your data by erasing and delete the storage, you need to know how to eliminate the information and assets required. Follow these steps to eliminate devices and data.

* Overwrite Data Overwriting: Data overwriting is a common method of eliminating data. It is typically used on magnetic disks. By overwriting the data by zeros or ones in several rounds it is possible to have data effectively erased. Each step reduces the recovery to zero.

* Degaussing is only used on magnetic disks. The process destroys the data and the disk. In actuality the device is subjected to a powerful magnetic field.

* Disrupt physical destruction of the devices. This is typically (but not always, if executed correctly) the most efficient method.

"Shred": It can be applied to magnetic tapes plastic devices, paper data. It's also identical to the destroy method.

Collection Limitation

It's a little tricky but it's a vital technique. It is simply saying that you don't store anything that is not needed. This can save time, space and also money. In the case of an organisation, it doesn't require a large amount of personal information from its employees. If someone is collecting this information, they need to secure storage, secure communicate and secure transfer the information while being clear about what is being collected. Laws and regulations in force today require those who collect data (i.e. websites) to get the approval of users immediately they arrive on their websites.

Chapter 6: Assure Proper Asset Retention

Archiving or keeping data can also pose a number of risk. Every organization must keep older data that is needed for the future. But, data that is at rest doesn't pose any risk like moving it or changing it. The principal risk here is double. In the event that data has been kept in storage that is not accessible it could pose physical danger from the device (e.g. degradation) or from people, as well as the environment. When the information is kept on the internet (for for instance Amazon Glacier) still it is not online. However, if it's online there is a chance of data transfer since there has to be assurance that the controllers and custodians will not alter or disclose information. Also, it is vulnerable to impersonation and other forms of attacks.

So, the retention strategies must be chosen with care. For instance, because of longer retention periods the technology used could become obsolete. If this happens data needs to be transferred to new devices and the cost must be reasonable. Some obsolete devices may corrupt data. Thus, a periodic routine is necessary to verify the data.

In all cases, regular checks, recovery trials and tests on physical devices (if an organization has them) are mandatory. When storing devices the location must be in line with regulations and standards. Physical damage can be prevented by having well-constructed rooms and controlled HVAC systems. Protection against fire as well as environmental catastrophes are important aspects to consider.

2.5 Determine the Data Security Controls

Learn to comprehend the Data States

Before you begin to apply data security it is essential to know the basics of data state. Let's examine the various states in which data may exist.

Data in rest Storage of data is not utilized

Data in motion The data is being collected, transferred or sent

Data used Actions or operations on data, such as changes and saving

Tailoring and Scoping

By scoping, the control options that fall within or outside the scope are identified. This is known as choosing the appropriate standards. Tailoring is the process of assembling (re-orientation as well as implementation and the development of) the controls in accordance with the needs.

NIST Security and Privacy Protections of Federal Information Systems and Organizations NIST Special Publication (SP) 800-53, Revision 4 offers a great guidelines for scoping and tailoring. The document is listed in the following.

By following the initial security baseline, you can identify and define the most common controls

- Scope determination and application

- Choice of compensation controls

assigning values to the security parameters for the organization (these are set by the company)

- Add additional controls to your baseline (enhancements)

- Supplying the specification of information necessary to carry out the controls

Standard Selection

This is a documentation process of selecting the standards for the organization-specific technologies or architectures that will be selected. It serves as a base for building upon over it. When building this the main focus is on the selection of technology instead of the selection of a vendor. Since the choice is made to meet the needs of diverse groups or people, the selection also caters to the requirements of new teams and individuals too. This means that it can be scalable and long-term sustainability.

There are a variety of widely recognized frameworks that you can choose from. Some of them were described in the previous sections.

OCTAVE OCTAVE

ISO 17999 and 27000 standards

COBIT - COBIT

- PCI-DSS

Data Protection Methods

A proper data protection method and tools must be used to safeguard the data at every stage. Let's take a look at this issue in greater detail.

Data at Rest Data at Rest: This is the data that isn't being utilized or transferred. There is a built-in memory protection feature built into several operating systems to prevent leaks and memory hijacking. For storage storage there's other security settings like encryption, access rights to the data and authorization details, as well as physical controls that restrict access to archives and hot storage. Storage based on WORM is also an media for storage (e.g. CD-R) and comes with integrity protection built-in, however it doesn't provide privacy (you need to utilize alternative methods).

Information is in motion (or moving) The data is being transferred to the computer's circuitry during use, or inside the network circuitry after transfer or accessed via remote methods. These types of data pose the greatest dangers. There are numerous security mechanisms, including TLS certificates, TLS encryption, and many more. In the case of remote access using VPN or RDS technologies There are a variety of security options, including public-key encryption, as well as VPN technologies. Additionally firewalls, as well as other devices are required to be set up in the areas around the remote devices and in. The remediation method will stop remote devices from connecting to the internet unless they are secure.

The data being used To safeguard the integrity of data that is in use, there exist a variety of operating system-level mechanisms that safeguard the memory of the working. Security mechanisms such as not security module for tamper protection kernel, address space processing isolating, physical segmentation buffer protection, protection of caches and extended protection with antivirus and web security.

In addition to these security measures keeping logs and auditing expose any threats and attempts on the operating system or memory. Monitoring logs and setting alerts can be proactive in preventing and detecting the attacks.

2.6 Establish the Information as well as Asset Handling requirements

The handling of assets requires the classification and labeling. The appropriate labeling applied to tapes, disks, and archives, which can help classify the equipment. This technique is applicable to all other storage device for data like disks, removable drives CD/DVDs, external hardware assets as well as storage cabinets for files.

Storage spaces must be equipped with adequate safety and security classification. They must be categorized according to the specific roles and the appropriate access and clearance mechanisms implemented. Access levels can be managed through labels or locking mechanisms, authentication , biometrics as well as any other pertinent controls.

As we have mentioned The deletion of information is the last phase of this procedure. This has been described in the previous section.

Chapter 7: Domain 3 - Security Architecture And Engineering

3.1 Implement and manage Engineering Processes utilizing Secure Design Principles

In this area we will look at the engineering aspects for security design. This is a very technical field unlike other domains.

A secure design is essential. it is crucial to establish a solid base from scratch when designing and developing strategies, resources like the software or other tools that are digital.

To remain within the security perimeter from the beginning it is essential that an organization adheres to the guidelines and standards set forth by security associations, governments as well as other relevant organizations. This will help reduce risk and avoids interoperability issues as well as compliance and problems with functionality.

This is a brief summary of the engineering procedure.

- Creating design concepts and ideas

Documenting and collecting the needs

- Feasibility Study and Specification of the requirements

- System design

Phase of implementation

Testing Tests are to be initiated at the level of the component and grow into modular test. The next step would be unit tests, beta and alpha tests, followed by user-experience studies. The final stage will include an entire test, that will be followed by scenario tests including simulations, scenario tests, as well as acceptance test. The designer will utilize an engineering platform as well as a testing platform specifically for engineering tasks. This ensures that the production system stays in place.

- Deployment

Training

Support and maintenance, including change management

3.2 Learn the Basic Concepts of Security Models

Security models function as a model, and allows the possibility of addressing security weaknesses by establishing security boundaries. CISSP students should be acquainted with the security models currently in use along with their pros and cons, and know the best way to implement them if needed.

Bell LaPadula (BLP) Model

Bell LaPadula model follows a state-machine model. It is a linear , non-discretionary model. It was later formalized as an element of the policy on multi-level security (MLS) which is a part of the U.S. Department of Defense. This model is designed to protect the issue of confidentiality. It includes the following features.

This type of model guarantees no-read-up and no write-down actions. It sounds like Greek? Let's clarify.

"No read-up (reading down) A person who has low-level clearance cannot read upper objects that require greater clearance.

No-write-down: A person with a higher level of clearance cannot record (attach or transfer) security objects to lower levels.

The model is guaranteed to be secure through the security measures that follow.

- Access: Prior to having permission to view, add, or execute the object specific protocol must be followed.

Access release: After the action has been completed and the access is released, it will be released.

Access to: A creator of objects allows an action to be carried out on his creation

Refuse access refers to the process of rescinding access after having granted an object (the opposite of giving access)

Make object: This protocol permits the creator to make an object active

- Remove object: The reverse of creating objects.

Change the Security level (below the level currently in effect)

One of the issues that is present in this BLP model is the absence of control of write-up. This is why it requires collaboration with other models.

Biba Model

This model fills in the weaknesses that were introduced by this BLP model. It actually guarantees no-read-down and zero-write-up. In this instance the person with higher clearance is unable to read from security objects of lower integrity. Additionally that a subject with lower integrity cannot write to objects that need higher integrity.

The Clark-Wilson Model is yet another model. The main purpose for this model's its integrity However, we're not going to explore the model in depth.

3.3 Make Selections Based on the System Security Requirements

This lesson is focused on selecting the controls based on the guidelines of a particular standard. Let's examine an illustration.

Common Criteria for Information technology Security Evaluation (A.K.A CC or Common Criteria) is an ISO/IEC standard for international standards. The standard was created in order to bring together the goals. The next order standards are incorporated into the standard. These are:

-- Information Technology Security Evaluation Criteria (ITSEC)

- Trusted Computer System Evaluation Criteria (TCSEC) - A.K.A. The Orange book, which is part in the Rainbow series

- Canadian Trusted Computer Product Evaluation Criteria (CTCPEC)

Let's take a look at the CC process in more detail.

Common standards cannot be used to judge hardware, but also software

The objective for the assessment (ToE) is to be determined first.

A security profile represents a particular collection of features necessary to ensure compliance with the standard criteria. Some vendors offer protection profiles that have certain limitations.

A security target, also known as an ST determines the security characteristics regarding the evaluation target

The entire evaluation procedure evaluates the level of confidence

Common criteria concentrate on the security assurance requirements. In order to achieve this the criteria defines seven levels of assessment assurance.

1. EAL1 Functionally evaluated

2. EAL2 Tested structurally

3. EAL3 is tested methodically and rechecked

4. EAL4: Methodically designed to be Tested, Developed and Reviewed

5. EAL5: Semi-Formally Created and tested

6. EAL6 Semi-Formally Verified Design Tested

7. EAL7: Verified in a formal manner and tested

3.4 Understand Security Capabilities of Information Systems (e.g., Memory Protection, Trusted Platform Module (TPM), Encryption/Decryption)

This section focuses on security features of hardware are being investigated for memory protection as well as Trusted Platform Module and encryption. Also, these are all hardware.

The first step is to be familiar with the concepts that are utilized in the design process.

Abstraction: Abstraction can be described as an approach to hide the presence of unnecessary components. This can help reduce the risk. For instance, if you write to a file on the computer you may not know which stacks are employed.

- Layering: Divides modules into layers. This can be done in conjunction with abstraction.

Domains for security Domains that restrict access at a to a certain level. Also, each domain is classified. This concept is often used to describe hardware. For instance, there's the model that is called the Ring model. It distinguishes between the Kernel mode from the user mode within an operating system, regardless of whether the virtualization is enabled or not.

Guarding the working Memory

Memory in computers (read-write or memory with random access) is used for the purposes of the kernel operating system and programs running on it. There are memory areas that only kernels can access. Some are reserved to the operating system. Memory leaks or hijacking processes may occur when a program, or even the operating system's component fails to behave as you would expect. For example in the event that a program trying to access an area of memory that is not allocated to it, the program or operating system could be unable to complete the task. In the end, this can become an attack.

The security measures listed below are accessible to all operating systems.

Hardware Segmentation refers to the process of dividing the hardware assets based on their importance of memory allocation.

Process isolation: isolating processes memory like virtual memoryor encapsulation and multiplexing, etc.

However, operating systems operate on the hardware we use, and even the assets of the company such as workstations and servers. Additionally, today the most sought-after device is smartphones. There are also risks to an organization if not controlled and adhered to standards.

Another option that is popular is virtualization. In this instance the hypervisor needs to be secured. There are two kinds of hypervisors.

Type 1. Operating system-level virtualization (VMware ESXi)

Type 2: These programs are run by OS, for example, VMWare Workstations, workstations and other local products.

Trusted Platform Module (TPM)

The module is a tiny chip that is integrated in a motherboard computer. Its primary function is to protect and supporting cryptographic operations.

The chip is capable of generating various cryptographic numbers and perform other security functions. Windows platform provides the service known as BitLocker. It makes use of the TPM to provide the highest level of security. This makes it much easier to secure and decrypt all of the hard drive. It's a great tool to safeguard privacy. There are numerous instances when TPM is utilized to provide security and protection against tampering.

Interfaces

The term "interface" refers to a link between two electronic equipment or between a person and a computer. In the case of a server-client operation in which a user would like to connect to the server through an interface will be employed. An example of this is the network interface card. It acts as an interface that connects the user to the motherboard. The other is the interface for email clients.

Interfaces must also be secured The following list includes them.

Encryption: This is usually used in conjunction with server-client systems. End-to-end encryption can be used to transmit data from client to server and vice back to protect against multiple attacks. A lot of mobile and web-based apps utilize encryption to safeguard users' interactions. If security is a concern There are VPN technologies that offer end to the end encryption, such as, IPSec, SSTP technologies. Remote desktop protocols offer similar levels of protection.

Failure tolerance refers to the capacity to withstand faults as well as the capability to continue to work in the event of an error. In this scenario it is recommended that a well-designed standby and backup systems are utilized.

Signing messages: This guarantees authenticity and the non-repudiation of.

3.5 Examine and mitigate the weaknesses of Security Designs, Architectures and Solutions Elements

Client-Based Systems

Client-based systems are the most vulnerable since the client's endpoints are utilized and controlled by the users. A client device could include a computer or handheld device. Since the majority of these clients are online at one point or another and are therefore quite susceptible.

A lot of users are not aware of the best practices for security. In addition to the actions they take is the following: the following items increase the scope of attack.

operating system as well as kernel security issues

- Updates are not being updated

- Software running decommissioned

- Installing numerous, unneeded software

Potentially undesirable applications

- Adware

- Malware

The majority of these problems arise because of a inadequacy of knowledge and understanding. In some instances, the absence of technical expertise is an problem. Even if devices are secure, users are still susceptible to psychological and social engineering attacks. The primary focus of any security program should be privacy and protection of the client. In addition to corporate security, safeguarding the individual client, they need to be safeguarded, being remediated prior to connecting to internal networks and safeguard remote users by implementing guidelines. To safeguard the internet it is recommended to use a commercial internet security suite is available. The majority of businesses purchase full corporate suites to meet needs.

Server-Based Systems

Servers inside the premises are secured the premises provided that adequate access controls within the premises and monitoring is set. Additionally, the accepted standards should be observed in the design of server rooms and when placing them. The backup generator, the fire extinguishers sensors, as well as emergency controls shield servers from physical attacks. Servers are also susceptible to insider threats by people.

Thus, following appropriate protocols and standards will ensure physical and logical security. In high-security settings (military and similar organizations) customized Linux/Unix operating systems are utilized to create security baselines. they also use customized configurations for security (i.e. access controls, such as discretionary controls) and layer access controls and authentication processes, end-point security with advanced firewalls and layered firewall technology, to stop DDoS attacks for servers that are able to accept internet-connected clients.

There are many kinds of threats that could harm servers if they're not regularly updated and inspected for security flaws. They could be internal weaknesses and known exploits, as well as internet-based attack on reconnaissance, as well as a myriad of other. Additionally, devices on the client can also spread threats if they aren't properly checked.

Database servers and servers on the web are also targeted frequently. There are advanced technology to analyze traffic incoming to detect patterns of attack. Some of these systems or software employ artificial intelligence to make the decision. Alongside these risks legitimate or unlegitimate traffic could overload servers. Load balancing devices are in place to handle the load and redirect traffic if required, or stop accepting requests in the event of an incident.

Certain networks employ IPS/IDS/Honeypot to protect themselves against cyber-attacks.

Databases

Databases are among the most vulnerable of services since they contain all of the important information. For attackers this is what they pay for most instances. A database could contain mission-critical information, Personal Identifiable Information (PII) such as customer data such as passwords, usernames, and other crucial information like credit card or payment information.

Operating systems also contain databases. For example, the credentials database within Windows is known as SAM (Security Accounts Manager) is a frequent attack target for hackers. But, it's difficult to break into such instances, however you need ensure that it is secured. SQL injection attacks are the biggest security threat to databases. Design flaws are the primary cause of these weaknesses. There are numerous tools to analyze websites and databases to see if they have security holes.

Cryptographic System

The field of study is techniques employed to conceal original data using mathematically generating random codes. The method of hiding it is known as encryption and the disclosure of it is known as decryption. A cryptographic system may be implemented within the company. In addition, there are many products available for implementing the system. But, there are weaknesses to these methods and systems.

Although cryptographic services are available but the software that relies on this could have weaknesses.

The encryption key has to remain secure (in length) and must remain secret. If it is asymmetric, it should be at least the length of 256 bits. However, the ideal size of 2048 bits. It is the encryption method that's crucial. Some algorithms might have been hacked or obsoleted.

Another crucial aspect is the protocol that is used. For example you can find security protocols, such as SSL, TLS, SSH, IPSec, and so on. Certain of them may be removed, while other protocols have been have been developed to be more robust.

Industry Control Systems (ICS)

A great illustration for the Industrial Control System is SCADA. SCADA is a short form in the form of Supervisory Control as well as Data

Acquisition. It is a system that can be used in an organization that is located within an established grid. Within the grid, there will be equipment, systems and software. Certain of these systems are serious security risks because the systems are outdated and utilize outdated technologies. They control national-level networks and an attack of a high-tech nature could destroy the entire system.

When it comes to attacks against ICS system, Stuxnet is a vital and the most effective penetration of the past. The virus targeted ICS systems of Iran's nuclear power stations. Another well-known malware attack is Duqu.

ICS systems typically operate in conjunction with the powerline systems. In these cases, they are a threat. This is why ICS systems need the highest degree of protection.

Cloud-Based Systems

There are many types that cloud-based systems can be built. These include,

Public cloud: Businesses contract out their infrastructure for a variety of advantages. The advantages include low maintenance costs and integration ease and high availability, and particularly leverage economies of scale.

Private cloud Private cloud: It is an version on-premise of cloud.

-- Infrastructure as a Service (IaaS): IaaS service providers offer infrastructure-level services and provide provisioning. They offer networking storage processing, memory and many other services, such as the ability to compute and flexible services. Amazon AWS is a good illustration.

Platform as a Service (PaaS) at this point, the support for development of applications as well as hosting are offered as an service. The infrastructure that runs the application is not managed, as IaaS. IaaS. It is handled by the company providing the services. One example is the Google App Engine.

• Software as a Service (SaaS) Cloud-based applications such as Microsoft 365, Google Apps and more.

-- Desktop as a Service (DaaS): DaaS is a new kind of service that offers remote VDI capabilities using the cloud (VID means Virtual Desktop Infrastructure).

Hybrid: A variety of hybrid service developed on top of popular service architectures.

The service providers manage cloud-based systems, with the exception of the time you buy IaaS solutions. IaaS system and control your box. Service providers take care of security and privacy , while also providing ways to keep availability as well as load management strategies. If an organisation relies on IaaS providers, they are responsible for the obligation to secure the infrastructure on their own, by installing firewalls as needed, DDoS protection, and other options.

If you decide to outsource the entire infrastructure, you will take a risk. You can't completely depend on remote methods. In the event that the internet backbone gets damaged it will be impossible to find an option to live. Thus, when selecting the cloud, organizations must think about a different backup option. Or, you can use the cloud for backup purposes. But, for purposes of archiving it's more appealing.

In all cloud-based environments authentication, authorization and accounting tools are readily available. With these features you can design solid and secure security, confidentiality, and non-repudiation capabilities. For example, Amazon AWS provides Identity and Access Management (IAM) capabilities. It also provides the various kinds of network security.

If you manage the cloud components by yourself it is your responsibility to ensure the security. If, for instance, you own a web server and you want to test for weaknesses, make backups and implement load balancing, DDoS protection and malware protection, adhere to the safest coding practices, and protect the backend service. There are a variety of tools available to try to hack your servers, perform vulnerability scans and security baselines.

If you manage cloud-based databases You must set up proper security mechanisms, validate the data, and prevent attacks by injection and ensure adequate backup and recovery systems.

Additionally, certain companies have to adhere to the requirements of compliance and regulations (e.g., HIPAA or PCI-DSS). In these cases they are accountable to adhere to these standards through collaboration with service providers, and creating the appropriate security policies. Furthermore, they are able to hire consultants and experts to assist them in the procedure. Another factor to consider is the transfer of services. In these cases it is essential to have skilled and technologically sustainable experts within the business. Consultants can be hired to help train and support the process of moving. Nowadays, service providers offer consultation services in their offerings.

Databases

You're aware that information and data are among the most valuable assets of an company. Databases that are internal and databases that receive queries from web servers are highly susceptible to attack. The majority of the time they are weakened because of inadequate security planning, absence of appropriate roles and permissions and auditing procedures and validation of data, absence of vulnerability scanning and security as well as the inability to review backups. These areas need to be taken care of and reviewed regularly.

Backups of databases are crucial to every operation. Backups need to be verified frequently and the practice of keeping offsite backups is strongly recommended. Offsite backups could be located in an alternative location, such as stored in the cloud.

Distributed Systems

These days, many web-based applications are spread across boundaries. When using these systems that are distributed, they aren't only the risks of environmental issues and the internet , but as well due to the transfer of data across borders. There are many options that are cloud-based, for instance as well as file-sharing services and web-based services. We covered security concerns as well as legal concerns associated concerning these systems in earlier sections.

Internet of Things (IoT)

IoT is a new and exciting area of applied technology. It is however an area where it is difficult to create a uniform security strategy. There are a variety of devices developed by various companies or even made from enthusiasts are available. For instance, there are numerous products created using Raspberry Pi. Some instances of IoT devices include wearables, health monitors and home management systems. They also include industrial and home security appliances for homes and powerline communication systems vehicles control systems, and payment systems.

The problem with a lot of devices is that they lack security measures from the beginning. Certain devices are not receiving regular updates or bug fixes, as well as security awareness, or a lack of authorization and authentication procedures. The primary reason is the lack of security management as well as access control. This is a major risk, which is the reason IoT isn't an option for every company. A thorough evaluation is needed in the event that an organization is open to incorporating these technologies within its operations. In addition, if it's difficult to control with the current policies the system must be dissuaded.

Chapter 8: Evaluate And Mitigate Vulnerabilities In Web-Based Systems

Web-Based Systems

A web-based system is any service, application, or device that relies on the web technology. Certain of these systems run on browsers as well as some software applications, such as mobile applications. Additionally, certain systems are based on an architecture that is client-server or a multi-tier structure.

Each of these systems is at risks, such as expanding the attack area. A majority of browser-based systems are vetted by the vendors of browsers as is the mobile app's validation by the app store's seller. But, with the sheer amount of extensions or applications the process is incredibly difficult. The most effective approach is to only use the essential and test its performance within the Sandbox. Furthermore developers should be reached out to learn about security architecture and benchmarks.

Web Servers

A Web server can be described as a typical workstation or server which runs the web server. A server-based system can employ either a single or multi-tier structure. As discussed in the preceding paragraphs, the web server need to be evaluated properly, and security safeguards should be installed. Code review is an additional important aspect. Furthermore, the validity of inputs from users as well as cross-site scripting vulnerabilities and many more must be identified.

Web servers should include malware detection and code mechanisms. They must also be able handle the high volume of traffic, and prevent false demands, DDoS attacks, and infrastructure malfunctions. We will examine the different threats to Web servers later in this following section. A security system for endpoints will be able to stop these attacks.

If you're already familiar with Open Web Application Security Project (OWASP) and its OWASP project, you might be able to better understand what web protection is and how important it is. To better understand this let's take an examination of the most frequent threats they identify each year following a substantial amount of research. The top Ten vulnerabilities are as follows.

- Injection

- Broken authentication

- Sensitive data exposure

External entities in XML (XXE)

- Access control control broken

Security configuration error

92

Cross-site scripting (XSS)

- Insecure deserialization

- Using software with known vulnerability

- Insufficient monitoring and logging

End-Point Security

Endpoint security is an element of a unified security management strategy. Endpoints are devices that has the capability of connecting to the network's internal network remotely. Endpoints may be the weakest link of an entire system, as discussed in various sections. So, any organization must take care to consider how it ensures the security of the endpoints. An integrated approach for an organization involves establishing internal security as well as remediation (to ensure that a system is current as well as free of infection and secure) encryption, as well as endpoint security. There are a variety of unifying and single-minded approaches to safeguard all systems from threats and weaknesses.

3.7 Evaluate and mitigate vulnerabilities in Mobile Systems

Mobile devices are gradually taking over laptops and computers in a rapid pace. The flexibility, mobility, speed of use, the long battery life, as well as the new technology for mobile networks enable the use of mobile devices, particularly when employees are moving around. A lot of companies permit users to Bring Your Own Device (BYOD) idea. The problem is diverse hardware platforms, various operating systems, the various versions, software repositories and security vulnerabilities. Recently, the environment is shifting. Developers are now focusing on a couple of major platforms, following standard processes when building hardware, and have even adopted a unifying security strategy. There are now capabilities to use security policies on any platform.

Mobile devices could be vulnerable to security risks since users are likely to install numerous applications and services both knowingly and inadvertently. In addition, Google and iTunes stores constantly remove fake applications from their stores.

However there are a variety of security features that aren't available on computers, for instance sensors, biometrics and sensors multi-factor authentication remote security, steal prevention, remote controls, as well as recovery methods. With all of these options and a secured administrators (root) account employed correctly mobile devices can outsmart computers in a variety of ways. There are a variety of uses that users can use, and they are more likely to engage in entertainment. These vulnerabilities open the door to attackers.

They can store financial information and also allows for the emergence of threats via the internet. Particular compliance requirements need to be satisfied prior to the mobile devices can be used to manage corporate accounts.

3.8 Assess and reduce vulnerabilities in embedded Devices

Many electronic devices come with the ability to connect to networks and connectivity. They pose a major risk since they do not pay attention to privacy and security. There are numerous electronic devices within the company including printers as well as scanners, networking gadgets, IoT devices, robotic and AI devices and more. In integrating these devices within your organization it is essential to analyze the design, find the weaknesses, and set appropriate and secure access and restrict their use to a specific set of functions. What makes embedded devices an imminent threat?

Embedded devices connect to developers' networks. The intention is to transmit crash reports, debug logs as well as user experiences. These ports are a welcome for attackers and should be either blocked or shut down.

Wi-Fi Protected Setup (WPS) is one of the connectivity options for numerous devices. As a default, routers offer these features (factory configurations). These features must be turned off since a malicious device could also access and monitor the networks via these gateways.

-- IoT is the next technology. The devices are not able to perform access management and cryptographic operations. So, the simple IoT isn't suitable for all organizations.

3.9 Apply Cryptography

The Life Cycle of Cryptographic Data (e.g. Key management algorithms selection)

Cryptography is a process that involves numbers, computational power and complexity in order to ensure that a document is protected from prying eyes. But, it doesn't guarantee security unless you utilize an integrated approach that includes an electronic signature.

The effectiveness of cryptographic functions is dependent upon the security of the key, the key size, and the space. Whatever the algorithm develop, their computational power grows quickly. This is a cause for concern among mathematicians because there are a variety of ways to compute and the computational power is due to multi-core, multiple-threading processors as well as Nvidia CUDA similar GPU cores. There are many ways to break into cryptographic keys, at the very least theoretically. The most significant security threat to the cryptographic key is the weaknesses in its algorithm.

It is essential be careful not to use low-quality cryptographic algorithms. There's a standard that is known by the name of Federal Information Processing Standards or FIPS. It was developed by NIST in line with the FISMA Act. In accordance with the guidelines, it is necessary to be wary of vulnerable algorithms (legacy or obsolete) and keys with weak lengths. While this is the case, there are limitations to using specific lengths of keys, based on the nature of the business.

Cryptographic Methods

Symmetric cryptography: major distinction between symmetric and asymmetric key encryption lies in the usage of one key. It is the same one used decrypt and decrypt using the symmetric method. In this instance you'll need possess a more lengthy key in order to ensure security. Also, you need an effective method of sharing the key to the other person.

Asymmetric key algorithm cryptography: This is a public key encryption method. In this approach it is the case that there's two key to be used. One is the private or secret key similar to the symmetric method. The other one is an open key, which means that anyone is able to access it and utilize it (it is accessible to the public).

Let's take a look at an example. It will also teach you the advantages of using an method of asymmetrical and how to secure the confidentiality, authenticity and non-repudiation.

1. If someone would like to send you secure messages (confidential) then he could encode the message using your private key.

2. You are the owner of access to the secret key. Only you and only you can access the private key. The message is accessible only if you decrypt it with an encrypted private key.

However, this does not assure authenticity and reliability. To accomplish this, you'll need the technique called Digital Signature.

1. To make sure that the person sending the message is actually the person, he encodes the encrypted message using the private keys of his own.

2. This will be attached and then sent to the person who received it. In certain cases the message will be included as a separate message in addition to the main message.

3. You must utilize his only private key for decrypting this. Because it's your public key you can be sure this person to be genuine.

In symmetric-key approaches this code is referred to as Message Authentication Coding (MAC). However, key sharing process can be difficult and cannot be leaked. So, MAC does not assure that it is not rescinded, whereas the digital signature does.

As you've probably guessed digital signatures guarantee authenticity, integrity and non-repudiation, while encryption guarantees confidentiality.

Within this segment, we'll be also examining Public Key Infrastructure (PKI) in detail. It is comprised of the following elements.

- - A Root Certificate Authority (RCA) server that has an option for backup (both are offline in the majority of cases)

A subordinate server set with backups

A collection of issuing CA servers that include backups

A set of policy CA servers

- Revocation list facilitation

There is a trust chain beginning with the server that is root. The root level certificate is the first step in the trust chain and is evident in the certificates issued. In order for a computer or digital device to be able to trust the root CA the certificate authority has to be trusted by the vendor as well as multiple different parties. This is especially important when the CA is public (internet-based).

If you've analyzed the certificate store of your computer there is a list of default certified root certification authorities as well as intermediate certificate authorities. There are names of the most popular and reputable certificate service providers, such as VeriSign, DigiCert, etc. There is also that the Microsoft Tamper Protection Root certificate in addition if you're running Windows.

A PKI should have certificate policies. Additionally, it should be able to provide an official CPS Statement of Policy (CPS). CPS statement describes how the PKI uses identities, how it will store keys, as well as how certificates are employed.

Certificates expire and need to be renewed regularly. A PKI must help with the process. Most importantly, it should cancel such certificates, and the revocation list should be made publically available.

Key Management Best Practices

The creation and distribution of keys The process of creating and distribution is private, the information exchanged must be protected, and must be maintained in the systems. Keys can be exported either with or without an encrypted key.

If you do export it using the private key, then you have to at a minimum password-protect the file.

- Protection and custody The keys need to be secured with a password or other method. If it's a high security or top-secret need or requirement, split custody may be employed. Only one of you owns a part of the access code and you must combine the other portion of the key that is owned by another person in order to open it.

Key rotation: It is crucial to rotate keys at certain intervals.

Keys destroyed: Key expiration and revocation should be handled in a particular way to avoid fraud and security concerns. operations. The list of revocations should be available to the public.

• Escrow: This technique is employed when a third party can gain access to the key. This method requires that the keys needed to decrypt or encrypt are stored in the escrow.

Backup and recovery This is the primary element of encryption. You should keep your private keys or symmetric keys safe. In certain situations, legislation might need access to your private keys. Nowadays, numerous PKI service providers provide methods for backup.

Digital Signature

This was already presented to you in an earlier section.

Non-Repudiation

Non-repudiation guarantees the non-denial of. For example, someone who sends a message will not later claim that he/she did not send it. they did not send the message. The problem is that it's impossible to know for certain whether the private key has been taken or is not.

Integrity

The subject was covered in the earlier section. It is possible to ensure integrity by hashing, authentication codes used in cryptography symmetrical, as well as digital signatures in the asymmetric cryptography.

Know the methods of Cryptanalytic Attacks

There are mathematical techniques and methods or strategies to crack encryption and cryptographic algorithms.

1. Text encrypted by ciphers in this scenario the attackers know the algorithm and the ciphertext that needs to be decoded.

2. A person who is known as a plaintext attacker is aware of this, and has either one or two plaintext-ciphertext pair created by an encryption key.

3. The attacker has chosen the plaintext. He is aware of the encryption algorithm used as well as the ciphertext and chosen plaintext along with the ciphertext that was generated with the key secret.

4. Chosen the ciphertext to the 3rd , but with the ciphertext being chosen by the attacker along with the plaintext decrypted by the key.

5. Chosen text: selected plaintext and the ciphertext combination.

Digital Rights Management

Rights can be defined, but it can be declared right and also the privilege. In the world of human beings it is a matter of favor for human rights. In a digital world, it is digital rights. In this context are applicable to objects. It is necessary to classify the object. The access to the object must be subject to authorization, clearance and authorization to perform certain actions with it. Furthermore, it must offer ways to share or distribute rights. Additionally, rights may be granted or removed. If the object is shared externally there should be two different rights, and each one must be managed in a separate manner.

There are numerous instruments and methods within the corporate world. They allow you to carry out the above-mentioned actions. Your rights are protected with certificates, encryption and other methods.

Chapter 9: Apply Security Principles To The Design Of Facilities And Sites

Within this segment, we'll examine the concept of facility design. Facilities design such as buildings, server rooms data centers, data centers, network operations centres, cable closets HVAC, and more.

If you've read this far, the layout of these facilities require an understanding of engineering and precise planning to ensure the entity. From the selection of land to land selection, there must be a strategy to manage risk. Location and location of land is crucial in avoiding any risk to the environment. For security reasons using natural resources is crucial. For example, for the purpose of securing a facility, it's important to think about urban camouflage. This can reduce the need for attraction. If the property has natural security, this can be a benefit. If you've ever visited an old castle you've probably seen how the structure is secured through surveillance and the natural surroundings.

It is important to take into consideration the territorial boundaries when you secure the partitions and areas that you have already built. Most of the time there will be restricted areas within the data centers, facilities servers rooms, etc. To gain access to these areas it is necessary to have access and clearance. It is possible to utilize cameras, signs as well as other means to deter people who don't have clearance from accessing the facilities.

One of the most crucial aspects to consider is control of access. In reality, it's more important than any other aspect. Facilities entrances can be protected by walls, fences as well as security guards and dogs, CCTV and other security measures as required. When designing access zones parking areas, standoff distances lighting, warehouse access security, and control systems have been carefully selected to be implemented, tested, and documented.

If you're looking at the reasons behind this the reason, it must be obvious that the primary goal is deterrence and reducing the impact of disasters (e.g. environmental effects).

If you are considering natural disasters, you need a strategy to ensure that the operation stays in operation. To fulfill the requirements of these, you need to ensure that backup sites are kept in an appropriate distance. A previous chapter discussed hot cold, warm and hot sites. These continuity options can be extremely beneficial in the case of a devastating catastrophe.

There are guidelines, approaches and guidelines to follow when building specific buildings like hospitals, health facilities laboratory, nuclear and various research facilities.

Crime Prevention through Environmental Design (CPTED) offers an integrated approach to reduce criminality through urban environment design and management. The primary purpose is to discourage offenders from engaging in crimes, and lessen the anxiety about

3.11 Implement Facility and Site Security Controls

This section we'll be investigating the internal facility operations, security, as well as risk reduction.

Intermediate distribution facilities and Wiring closets

The IT infrastructure is laid out in the process of building the facility (in the building stages). There will be a variety of cables enclosures, wires, and enclosures that will be aplenty. All wires or ends will be tucked away inside a casing or room. There are many dangers for the wires. If they are exposed in the ground, workers could harm them. If there's a possibility of fire from the heat source, it may cause damage to the wires. If the cables for network connections are located near power lines, they could cause interfering. Most importantly, if cables are not secure and visible to people any person can initiate an Man in the Middle (MitM) attack. So, the closets should be locked down to a certain group of technicians. To protect access, they are granted access with a fingerprint or another biometric verification.

Server Rooms/Data Centers

An in-house server room as well as an data center, which includes multiple hardware devices servers, like racks for servers, require extremely precise and secure design and construction principles. You must adhere to certain guidelines for environmental conditions, interior design guidelines, numerous regulations for compliance, and often get legal clearance.

It should be constructed in a location in which natural disasters (potentials) are low. External safeguards should have been put in place. To gain access to it, there should be a documented, specific procedure. The level of clearance should be specified in conjunction with the design. Controls for access using biometric devices are essential in this situation.

The interior rooms should be constructed to manage humidity, heat and dust. It should use sensors to avoid electric surges, overheating, the occurrence of fire, wetness, or static electricity. The design has sophisticated and modern controls that can be used to complement the design, which includes sophisticated HVAC controls.

A strict monitoring system is necessary both inside and out of the entrance to the facility. Even if the technicians are granted authorization, their actions must be monitored accordingly.

Additionally to these needs, a continuous energy supply, as well as generators to provide backup power are essential. The circuitry needs to be protected from lightning strikes and surges.

Data Storage Facility/Media Storage

Media storage facilities are an advanced area inside the server room. It could also have additional surveillance systems. It could also be more frequently accessed. Thus, the same considerations regarding controls are in place.

Restricted Work Zone

A work zone that is restricted is a zone that is reserved for missions-critical activities. In certain situations, employees could or not be working in the area. One example is the server room, the Network Operations Control Area (NoC) or vaults, or even the laboratory. Access control and monitoring is required in this instance. Auditing is also required to protect assets from internal threats.

Utilities and HVAC

As mentioned in the preceding section, air-conditioning, ventilation, and heat are vital environmental control systems. It provides a specific atmosphere for the critical equipment to work and for people to perform their work and also facilities that meet requirements (e.g. laboratories, for instance.).

These systems are crucial when it comes to risky operations like power stations that use nuclear energy. In these instances modern technology and precision clinically is needed to maintain the temperature, the ventilation (heat controlling) and coolants in check.

In the server room, it is essential to be able to control humidity levels in order to prevent corrosion, airflow, and air conditioning to keep the air dust, temperature, and temperature under control.

In all of these scenarios you should also think about backup power to run the process or to shut it down at the right time in case HVAC fails to supply electricity. In all instances the devices and controls are to be monitored and monitored within a certain time.

Environmental Issues

As we have seen in numerous sections, environmental issues and natural disasters are a part of the human experience. They are beyond our control and it is imperative to plan how to get back from an event. This is the reason why the selection of the land and its surroundings is essential. The proper considerations should be made in the next.

Natural disasters such as flooding, forest fires eruptions of volcanic ash, and similar problems.

Fires can cause destruction to entire areas. Based on the kind of fire, or cause of the fire, the appropriate safeguards like fire extinguishers or suitable water sources should be present. In the event of a risk the fire is at, there may be several types of fire extinguishers.

There are extreme weather conditions like floods, heavy rains tornadoes, hurricanes, and lightning.

A special consideration should be given to designing and building structures that will withstand the rigors of natural disasters like earthquakes. You can mitigate physical harms with proper plans for construction and architectural designs.

Prevention of fire, Detection, and Suppression

In this article we will take a look at various protection against fires, fire detection and suppression techniques and methods which must be put in place in the facilities.

To avoid a fire The first step to prevent a fire is to consider design aspects. When designing the facility the proper analysis and documentation is required for the materials used such as electrical power cables, outlets air conditioning and ventilation spaces and fire-sensitive structures such as exit points and crucial points at which fire suppression may be difficult.

In the following stage when designing process, fireproof materials, techniques and possibly prevention control methods must be used. For example, certain materials could be used to build walls that stop fire from occurring.

At this point it will be possible to create technologies that detect and report on fire and other incidents. This aids in preventing and in detecting fire. There are sensors for fire such as temperature monitors, temperature monitors, alarms, sensors cameras, and alarms that can be utilized in a holistic manner to stop and detect fire. These devices work together in preventing, swiftly recording, and reporting fires. The goal of any incident, is confine the fire and restrict the fire to a smaller, but manageable area and avoid affecting vulnerable zones.

There are a variety of techniques for reducing fire. A company must use multiple techniques when the building and its assets exhibit distinct responses to fire. In the case of fire, for instance. You could stop a fire using water, however, if it is oil-based, then you need to choose an alternative suppression device. The following types of suppressors can be put in areas that have easy access.

Water - Water

- Gas suppressors , such as FM200 are ideal for datacenters

- Foam-based suppressions

- Halon-based suppressors

- Water-mist

- Sand

Chapter 10: The Domain 4 - Communication And Network Security

All things are interconnected and that's the reason why you should have an entire section on this issue in your CISSP studies , as the most significant security threats are transmitted via networks. For students who are comfortable with networks or have a system or network administration experience, this chapter should be a simple investigation. However, if you're unfamiliar with specific technology, it's the right time to take a short course. This chapter explains ideas are explained in a way that you can comprehend even if you have small amount of knowledge.

4.1 Apply the Secure Design Principiale in Network Architecture

Open System Interconnection (OSI) and Transmission Control Protocol/Internet Protocol (TCP/IP) models

The network architecture was built on two main models. These are the foundational elements of the communications networks which are in use today. These models are

- OSI model

Model TCP/IP

ISO/IEC7498 can be described as the theoretical model. It is, in actual an accepted model. It is a seven-layer structure for establishing communications between two devices or computers within a network. The idea behind this model is to simplify and make it easier to understand.

Then, a simplified variant of the ISO layer was developed and is referred to by the name of TCP/IP. This model was the foundation for the interconnectivity over the internet. This model is employed with nearly all internetworking and outside networking designs.

Let's take a look at a comparison to better understand the different models. Below each model's layers, relevant protocols are identified.

IP Internet Protocol Networking

Internet protocol is actually the basis of network interconnection and the way to address. The protocol allows for the communication of protocols.

Let's take a look at the features of IP. It's a non-connexion protocol. This means that it doesn't require prior agreements. Also, it is referred to as an unstated protocol since it is not able to determine what time a conversation started. To ensure reliable communications, it utilizes its transport layer protocol TCP. TPC is actually is a reliable, connection-oriented protocol. The security is ensured through the use of sequence numbers for packets, as well as buffering and error correction.

The other protocol for transport layer is known as the Universal Datagram Protocol. It's also a non-connectionless protocol. The IP protocol can be used in conjunction with this one as well. Because it doesn't need specific actions and orientation for connections it's extremely fast.

In the present it is 32 bits of IP address currently being used. It was previously known as TCP/IP version 4. The latest version of the protocol is Version 6. It comes with the address space 128 bits.

Another crucial concept to know about is socket. When two devices are connected through a socket, for example creating two sockets. Each protocol is assigned a port number. There are various ports that have identifications. These are:

- System ports that are well-known and known Ports ranging from 0 to 1023 are reserved for system services

Registered Ports IANA reserve 1024 to 49151. On request, it may be reserved.

Private and unusual ports Ports 49152-65535 may be connected to popular ports and complete any development work.

The implications of multilayer protocols

There are various types of protocols. Certain of them can be single layer protocol and others are multilayer protocols. Multilayer protocols use several TCP/IP and OSI layer. For example, the Asynchronous Transport Mode or ATM switching technique employed by telecommunications service providers employs this method. In actual fact, ATM uses three layers for operation. It uses these layers concurrently. In order to combine three layers it makes use of an encapsulation method. The data of the top layer is then encapsulated by lower layers process it. It also adds an extra header to the data, also known as an additional trailer or header. ATM is utilized to create Synchronous Optical Networking (SONET). SONET can be used to transfer large quantities of high-priority data such as videos and voice via long-distance networks.

Converged Protocols

In this scenario it's a combination between two protocol. Most of the time, it is a proprietary protocol as well as it is a standard protocol. This is a major benefit since it eliminates the need for changes to infrastructure and upgrade. Particularly when catering to multimedia requirements and requirements, this can be extremely economical. In reality, safeguarding as well as scaling and managing the same is much simpler than implementing the use of a private network. However, mixing different protocols and technologies can create security issues. However, by leveraging the security features already present in protocols, it's not difficult to come up with one unified strategy.

A few instances of convergenced protocols include,

-- Fiber Channel over Ethernet (FCoE)

- iSCSI

- MPLS

SIP (used in VoIP operations)

Software-Defined Networks

Software-defined networks were created through the introduction of cloud computing and virtualization services. They replicate the physical networks and operates more precisely in certain situations. They are designed in order to address problems like budgetary issues, adaptability problems as well as flexibility, scalability and flexibility through the addition of more dynamic features and the ease of use. Let's review some of the characteristics included in SDN.

Agility: It offers an abstract control over forwarding. This provides administrators with a massive advantage by allowing them to alter the flow of traffic to meet changing requirements in a dynamic manner.

Centralized Management: SDN controls, it is centralized network intelligence is maintained that provides an overview of all networks. Also, it acts as a switch for application and policy engineers.

Programmability SDNs are directly programable. This is due to the separation from forwarding functions.

- Vendor Neutrality and Openness

Programmmatic Configuration: This is the fundamental nature of SDNs and that is the reason why they was so well-known. Network professionals can configure and manage, optimize and protect resources in a dynamic manner or through automation.

Wireless Networks

Wireless networks were the main mode of communication but in the present wireless networks have evolved into more difficult and in some instances, more lucrative as compared comparison to wired networks. In the age of mobile devices wireless networking as well as wireless broadband networks are among the possible alternatives on handhelds. Alongside broadband, wireless services accelerate rapidly by expanding their capabilities. Wireless networks adhere to an IEEE 802.11 standard.

Wireless Security Protocols

There are many wireless security protocols and the CISSP student should be equipped with an understanding of them to ensure that the most effective of the bunch can be incorporated into the security plan.

Wired Equivalent Privacy: WEP is an old and outdated security protocol, and was the preferred protocol for a while. It was removed because of security vulnerabilities inherent to it. The WPA standard family replaced it. WEP employed RC4 for security and CRC-32 for checksums to ensure authenticity. There were various versions like the 256, 64 and 128, however, they did not have WEP keys. In the end, a method was devised to locate WEP keys using encryption.

Wi-Fi Protected Access (WPA) It uses the Temporal Key Integrity Protocol (TKIP). It creates a 128-bit encryption key for each packet. It also performs integrity tests. Unfortunately, WPA inherited a weakness that was discovered in WEP that allowed that it be used to spoofe as well as reinjection attacks.

-- WPA 2. Different from WEP and WPA, WPA2 provides strong security and encryption to protect your data. It is compatible with Advanced Encryption Standard (AES) If the client isn't supported it will provide TKIP support. In general it is possible to specify an encrypted key that is pre-shared, however it's not recommended for an enterprise setting. In these situations it is compatible with the use of certificates to authenticate.

-- WPA version 3 It is the next version of the WPA2 standard and is the replacement to the. WPA 3 uses the latest security protocols, eliminates the old and ineffective requirements for using of Protected Management Frames (PMF). It also provides natural password choice, convenience of use, as well as forwards security even after a password breach. The features for enterprises include authentication-based encryption (256-bit) as well as verification and derivation of keys (HMAC-SHA384) Key establishment, the ability to authenticate (ECHD, ECDSA with the 384-bit Ellipsic curve) and Robust management frame security (BIP-GMAC-256).

Alongside these wireless protocols, the systems incorporate certificate infrastructures and certificates as well as other protocols, such as TLS or IPSec. In some companies the Wi-Fi Protected Settingup or WPS is employed. Because of the vulnerability and the risks that come to it, the use of it should be avoided.

4.2 Secure Network Components

Computer networks are the fundamental foundation of communication for any business. Network components make up the network's backbone. to secure the network from the beginning these components must be secured.

Operation of Hardware

In order to build a network, an array of components must be connected. We'll look at the peripherals and devices such as monitors, detectors load balancers, and detectors.

Concentrators and Multiplexors These devices serve to combine or multi-channel digital signals. FDDI is an illustration

Modems and Hubs Modems were utilized earlier to switch digital to analog and vice reverse. Hubs are used to build networks of a certain type or to create specific topologies. For example the ring or star topology. They are mechanical devices with no intelligence or decision-making capabilities. Additionally hubs are only a single collision domain and is not trustworthy nor secure.

Layer-two Devices: These devices function within layer two of OSI level two. You already know that this is the layer that handles data. Bridges and switches both function within this layer. Bridge networking is the case where architectural similarity is needed between two devices, like. It's also not able to stop attacks that could occur within an individual segment. However, the switch is more effective and most importantly it separates this collision area and allocates ports. Additionally, the switch comes with a port-security feature as well as authentication, VLANs and much more.

Layer-three devices They operate over that layer, which is known as the data link. So, expect higher-quality and more efficient devices. Layer 3 units provide collaborative system that connects different devices. They allow the devices to be connected and also to work together. The router as well as the layer 3 switch are two of the most popular examples. Layer 3 devices are a great source of security options, as well as configuration and control. For instance, you could purchase devices that offer advanced authentication techniques including firewalls, security features, support for certificate services and many more.

Firewalls are the primary player in the realm of security for networks. In an enterprise setting firewalls work as a tiered structure. They serve as a packet filter , but it makes intelligent choices regarding packet forwarding. A firewall employs two strategies. The first is static filtering while the other is a stateful inspection. The latter is more beneficial because it bases the decision in the context.

Transmission Media

There are numerous transmission media used in various situations. The following list provides the various transmission options.

Twister pair

Shielded twisted pair (STP)

Unshielded twisted pair (UTP)

- Coaxial cables

Fiber optics

- Microwave

- Powerline communication

The cables that are twisted can be laid across different parts of a structure. In these situations cables can end up or pass through unintentional places. If this happens it is likely that a Man-in-the Middle incident (tapping) is likely to happen. If shielding is not adequate copper cables are susceptible to radiation and interference. So, the cables should be laid out with care.

Copper cables are susceptible to similar problems. For example, Coaxial cables are bulky and difficult to use. Like twisty cables, they have the potential to be damaged by tapping, but with they are less susceptible to interference. Because of the shielding, they may be protected against fire, but not always.

It is one of the safest and untappable medium. It also has a large bandwidth regardless of whether the cable is multi-mode or single. Multi-mode does not have bandwidth, however both models are well-managed.

Network Access Control (NAC) Devices

Like the name implies the concept of network access control is like a watchdog that guards the perimeters. These devices could provide physical and physical controls as well as logical ones.

Firewalls: This topic is discussed in a separate section.

-- Intrusion Prevention Systems/Intrusion Detection Systems/Honeypots A Honeypot or IDS device is an security device that is able to detect threats in the real world or attacks that take advantage of the assets. IPS however, on the other hand, seeks to stop attacks before they take place. In reality, IPS devices or controls offer real-time alerts and updates. Honeypots are a virtualized network that exists within a simulation. The simulator is able to open ports and reveal weaknesses, so that attackers are not misled. It is used for protection as well as gather information about attack vectors.

Proxy/Reverse proxy forward proxy is a device that intercepts the traffic of the internal network, and then screens specific information for external third parties. For example, PII information. It also has the ability to filter out traffic. A reverse proxy blocks traffic that is coming in. In this case, it can offer caching, load-balancing, and attack mitigation.

End-Point Security

We've discussed more about end-point security in the previous chapters. To protect end-point devices. In addition to the security measures using security policies that include auditing rights management, auditing and remediation networks remote access protection safe VPN as well as RDS solutions, unidirectional web security suites, firewalls that are hosted are among the most important concerns.

The next step is to follow best techniques. Employees might not have sufficient information about the company's security plan and its technical areas. They need to be trained through exercises and training. A solid base of knowledge for them is an additional aspect. Alongside these operations, there are corporate-managed ones and limitations, such as

Automated updates and patch management

Devices restrictions, for example the prohibition of bringing devices that are removable in or out and implementing policies on media

- Restricting administration and application capabilities

Content Distribution Networks

The content distribution network, or a CDN is a network that is designed to deliver bandwidth-consuming content with no delays to end users across diverse geographical areas. Also, it improves the user experience. It eliminates delays for downloads or uploads and reduces the time spent. Some examples are Cloudflare CDN and Amazon CloudFront.

There are many ways to contaminate the caches and the caches must have adequate restrictions in place. It provides, for instance, security for data through Identity and Access Management, restricting access to original content using other methods such as compliance and monitoring, DDoS mitigation using field-level encryption and many other features that ensure the security of users.

Physical Devices

If security that is logical is the main security concern, what is physical security? Similar to the practices of network security physical security is an important issue. In fact, it's more important than anything else the majority of the time. To safeguard the physical devices in an organization suitable measures, such as physical and logical monitoring cameras, sensors, and sensors are able to be installed. Secure access control mechanisms (keycards or codes, biometrics) as well as scanning can be beneficial methods to prevent physical damage as well as theft and unauthorised access.

A lot of devices have physical locks today to protect against theft of devices. In this scenario devices will become secured. In addition to devices like laptops, computers, mobile devices such as smartphones, laptops and other devices are also susceptible to theft. They should be secured by using all available security features including encryption and screen locks, password protection as well as hard drive locks. remote access, and management including remote wipes and security policies that can be utilized to restrict access to devices that are not authorized.

4.3 Create Secure Communication Channels according to the Design

This section we'll examine secure communication methods that can be employed within an organization to safeguard the data that is in motion.

Data communication Secure communication channel can be one that is either internal or as an external channel through which secure communications can occur. If the communication is conducted internally, there should be separate channels in order to keep the channels of communication secure. One of the best examples is the Virtual LAN or a VLAN in short. VLANs are a great way to protect your network and provide security, while also ensuring the communications between the parties. In addition to internal communications external communications can be secured by using protocols like IPSec as well as TLS.

Multimedia collaboration: Workplaces aren't restricted to voice and text activities anymore. There are a myriad of collaboration tools that can be used in daily activities. Many activities make use of text or voice recordings, and shared resources in order to accomplish tasks, communicate with people, and for training as well as public occasions. Web conferencing and webinars can be effective ways to learn and share information. Numerous collaboratives tools provide the capability to organisations including schools, campuses as well as other organizations. These tools include Microsoft 365, ERP tools like SAP, Adobe Connect, Google Apps, Cisco WebEx, Freshworks (helpdesk), Slack, Skype, virtual meetings and virtual classroom solutions and other web-based conferencing tools are all available. If you are using these tools it is essential to ensure that they are secure for communication as well as infrastructure security and conformity. For example, a conferencing toolcalled "Zoom," is criticized for being unsecure in the beginning of 2020. It is possible that WebRTC as well as other applications might require further developments in the security field. Protocols like RTMP can be secured by implementing custom protocols.

Remote Access: You can use numerous protocols that can provide safe access for your company remotely. They include SSH, VPN technologies, Remote Desktop Services (RDS), Remote Desktop Protocol, VNC as well as other. The decision-making process should focus on encryption from end to end as well as infrastructure security and conformity requirements. Furthermore, transborder restrictions should be taken into consideration. A lot of these tools are compatible with certificates and are employed to secure communications through TSL or other methods. Other services, like RADIUS, are used to authenticate users with certificates or other mechanisms.

Furthermore, every authenticated computer or device has to go through an authentication network in order to ensure the security and compatibility.

In the case of virtual infrastructures, such as virtual Desktop Infrastructures Hypervisors as well as other products provided by companies like VMWare and Microsoft there are certain concerns regarding security. These infrastructures and VDIs should be running the appropriate security software to safeguard the sessions. Additionally the services need failover configurations to ensure that they are accessible.

Voice and Video Videos and voice create an impact on engagement and can bring great success to companies. In the present, companies of all kinds have used collaboration tools as well as third-party tools to communicate with stakeholders, customers and customers as well as handle internal communications, meetings and training. As previously mentioned they are essential solutions (QoS which is also known as the quality of services) and require large bandwidths. Most of the time, they are provided through tunnels and specialized infrastructure (on the internet). In the list of applications, Instant Messengers are among the best. Some examples are Skype, WhatsApp, IMO, Viber, and there are other enterprise tools like Microsoft Teams, Skype for enterprise, Adobe Connect, Cisco WebEx, and many other collaborative, virtual conferencing/webinars/classrooms. These services offer end to ending encryption in many cases , as well as privacy services. When integrating, however the design of end-to ending encryption, privacy, and other regulations must be followed. Certain countries don't allow these toolsand, as a security professional you should be aware the issues.

Chapter 11: It Security And Career

This section is that is aimed at those who are considering an occupation with IT Security or starting their career in this field. What are the best ways to create a successful career within IT Security in the document in this section, we will explore the reasons why IT Security experts have so numerous demands in the present. The goal will be to review the most sought-after IT Security certificates in order to determine the best path for reaching your goals in this field as well as to advance your job prospects in the CISSP field.

IT Security History in Brief

The background of IT Security dates back to the 1960s. In the beginning, we will discuss five reasons why you should consider working in this field, before going through the entire process of its past.

1. Demand Increasing

As the increasing number of successful attacks the need for skilled professionals working in the field of IT Security.

2. Job Garanty

When you begin you career path in the area of IT Security, as long as you're effective in your work and are productive and efficient your job security will be there for you to ensure that the demand for skilled employees in this field is very high.

3. With Multiple Areas within Its Own

Because it is true that the IT Security field is divided into several areas within it You are likely to locate a job that is suitable for your skills or experience, as well as your interest, personality and goals for your career.

4. Take a leap in your Career

The more you are involved in the area of IT Security and become productive within your area and enhance your knowledge and practice, it's much simpler to obtain the required certificates and rise into the top positions as compared to other professional groups.

5. The Financial Impacts of the New Economy

In the "Burning Glass Cyber Security Jobs" report released at the end of 2015 it was stated that those working within IT Security earned more than workers in other IT areas.

Let's say we look at the evolution of IT Security history with important particulars;

1969:

First message sent via ARPANET.

-- ISACA was founded.

1975

The initial testing of the TCP / IP protocol for data communication was conducted on both networks.

1983:

- ARPANET began to implement TCP / IP. TCP / IP protocol.

1985:

the first reliable Windows version Microsoft, Windows 1.0 has been released.

1986:

-- "Computer Criminal and Fraud Act" law was approved as a law by United Nations Congress.

1988

-- Robbert Tappan is written by Morris, Morris Worm. The first instances concerning the risks of using the Internet have been revealed.

So the CERT-CC (Emergency Response Team Coordination Centre) was founded by the USA.

First major networks operation was completed.

1989:

-- SANS Institute was established.

1990:

Internet was born. Internet

1993

First DEFCON Conference was held.

1996:

- HIPAA was created.

2004:

-- PCI DSS has been installed.

2005:

-- ISO document have now been made public.

Workstations

The rapid growth of technology opens up new possibilities for institutions, companies and even individuals. Although this is beneficial in many ways, it has also has also brought new dangers. If we take a look at a broad range of IT Security, Cyber Security is a sector which has emerged to minimize the risks posed by technology advancements. Thanks to the advancement of technology and new technology, there are emerging technologies to store large amounts of data, and organisations and institutions trying to make the transition to technological advances produce a lot more data and utilize more complicated software. In addition, they are situated in a highly risky environment, such as the Internet. This is why companies require IT Security experts to ensure their data security and be aware of potential risks to their businesses prior to.

When we consider all cyber-attacks which have been conducted to date it is evident there are many attacks that have been carried out, in addition to the organization that is the primary victim, they affect a variety of organisations, institutions and even people who work for it in a negative way. The increase in attacks has increased the significance of cyber security in the private and public sectors, which led to the requirement for staff in the area cybersecurity. This is why it's important research has been conducted to prepare personnel for work in the area of cyber security in a number of countries, which includes in our country.

In the context of the National Cyber Security Strategy and Action Plan within our country the "Cyber Star" contest was held through the National Cyber Incidents Response Center (USOM) which is a part under the Information Technologies and Communication Authority (BTK). The Cyber Star Contest is designed to connect people who have an interest in and a capacity for cybersecurity, and to provide participants with an chance to grow, and to spread awareness about the field in our nation. Additionally cyber security training camps are organized to recruit qualified professionals into the field by firms that have the highest percentage of success in this area.

As BGA as BGA Information Security ACADEMY, in an effort to fill the gap of qualified personnel in this field and help in the realization of our nation's National Cyber Security vision, since 2011 it will be offering two times each year that we offer a program for students who are interested in pursuing the career of "Cyber Security" and to focus on this area. We are implementing "Cyber Security Camp". More than 22,000 applications have been submitted in these Cyber Security Camps we've completed to date. Through these applications over 250 students were taught with the Cyber Security experts. They were brought to the industry in the future and continue to be taken in.

Career in IT Security

There are numerous career opportunities that are available in IT Security. In this article we will discuss nine major business categories. We will discuss the requirements, experience and the certifications needed to work in these categories. Naturally this will be the most important issues. These job titles are separated into sub-titles such as junior expert, and expert experts. It is worth noting that Information Technology, Computer Engineering as well as Computer Engineering. for those who intend to get their start in this area in general. It is said that they must graduate from these areas. Although this may bring the person one step further in first, when the individual has made progress in this area and has obtained the required certifications, the field in which in which he graduated won't be of any significance. Since you possess a fascinating pattern of informatics that are vital in this area,

Information Security Specialist Technologist

Job description:

* Design, tests and displays security configurations of systems and networks.

* It safeguards systems from access by unauthorized persons or modifications.

* Conducts weakness analysis and tests.

Business Titles:

* Data Security Specialist

* Cyber Security Expert

* Security Specialist for Computers

* Security Consultant for Networks

The Skills that are required:

* Get detailed information about TCP /IP computers, computer networks, switching and routing.

Get detailed information on Windows, Unix and Linux operating systems.

* Be knowledgeable about security technology and processing techniques (IDS / the IPS system, penetration tests etc.).

Find out more information about ISO 2700/27002, ITIL and COBIT frameworks.

Certificates:

* CEH

* CISSP

* Security +

Job experience:

* Beginning Level: 1-2 years

*For Expert Level 5or more years

Salary Band:

* Based on the studies carried out in the USA the results have been found that the average annual earnings are $ 81,000 per year.

* Analyst in Information Security

Job description:

* His professional experience uses weaknesses to detect dangers and risks.

* It displays and monitors tracetraces of the network for IT Security.

* Examines current threats by using tools for cyber security.

* Performs extensive studies on security-related events.

Business Titles:

* IT Security Analyst

* Clarity Analyst

* Pentest is

* Incident Response Analyst

* Security Risk Analyst

* Auditing Analyst

Essential Skills:

* Analytical abilities should be enhanced.

* Verbal and written communication skills must be improved.

* Problem solving skills must be developed.

* Programming language knowledge (Python, PERL, Windows PowerShell, etc.) must be at a high level.

Certificates:

* CompTIA A +, Network + and Security +

* CISM

* CISSP

Job experience:

* He must have the necessary training and experience in a related field to IT.

* He should have 5-9 years of work experience in the position he is applying for.

* You should be skilled in taking swift action in traffic analysis.

Salary Band:

* In the research conducted in the USA the results have been established that the annual income is $ 84,000.

• Information Security Auditor

Job description:

* Plans and oversees security audits.

It also provides audit reports either verbally or in written form.

It conducts audits to enhance security across all sectors.

Business Titles:

* Auditor for Information Security

* Information Systems Auditor

141

* IT Auditor

The Skills that are required:

* Organizational skills must be developed.

* Written and verbal communication skills must be developed.

* Should have all the details about operating systems.

* He must be knowledgeable about security systems (firewall IDS, firewall.).

Certificates:

* CISA

* CISM

* CISSP

Job experience:

* Computer Engineering, Information Systems Engineering, Management Information Systems etc. must have been able to graduate from the departments.

* He should have at least 5 years of experience with consulting firms, preferring to be known as 4 senior.

* Know about ISO 27001/27002, ITIL or COBIT frameworks.

Salary Band:

142

* Based on the studies carried out in the USA the results have been found that the average annual earnings are $ 83,000 per year.

* Contact Information Security Consultant

Job description:

* It helps protect the system optimally against attacks that could be able to compromise the system.

* It discusses security concerns with employees of the department.

* Evaluates weaknesses and analysis of risk.

Business Titles:

* Contact Information Security Consultant

* Consultant in Computer Security

• Database Security Consultant

* Consultant for Network Security

* Cyber Security Expert

Essential Skills:

* Organizational skills need to be developed.

* Writing and verbal communication skills must be developed.

* Experience with network and system (preferably Unix and Windows 2003/2008/2012) is required.

Security Systems (firewall IDS, Firewall, etc.) are a must.

Certificates:

* GIAC certificates (GCIH, GCFE, and GCFA)

* OSCP

* CSC

* CPP

* PSP

* CISSP

Job experience:

* It is preferential to hold a degree in a field like Computer Science, Computer Engineering.

* Must have at least 2 to 4 years of work knowledge in the area.

* ISO 27001/27002 requires ITIL and COBIT previous experience.

Salary Variation:

* Based on the research carried out in the USA the results have been found that the income per year is $ 101,000.

• Information Security Engineer

Job description:

* It creates innovative technological solutions.

It also conducts assessments and examines how new technology will impact the security programs for the organization.

The software installs and sets up security infrastructures.

* Writes scripts.

* Examines security-related incidents.

Business Titles:

* Engineer in Network Security

* Engineer in Information Security

* Information Systems Security Engineer

Essential Skills:

* Knowledge of operating systems must be excellent.

* System for Security (firewall IDS, firewall.) are a must.

* Secure coding skills must be built.

* Must have complete information on virtual technologies.

Certificates:

145

* CEH

* GIAC certificates (GCIH, GCFE, and GCFA)

* CCNP Security

* CISSP

Job experience:

* It is preferable that he be a graduate of Computer Science, Computer Engineering.

* Should have been for the IT field for at least 5 years. You must also have worked within the IT Security field for at minimum 3 years.

* He must have adequate expertise in technology such as routing and switching, IP address DNS.

* You must have a thorough understanding regarding operating systems.

Salary Band:

* In the research conducted in the USA it was found that the average annual income of the US is $105,000 per year.

The Information Security manager

Job description:

Controls access to the system.

Network monitors applications and security of data.

Monitors the flow of traffic.

It safeguards the system against unauthorised access.

Business Titles:

* System Security Manager

* Network Security Manager

• Information Security Manager

Essential Skills:

Have complete information on protocols like TCP or IP, SSL, TLS, HTTP, DNS, SMTP and IPsec.

* Should have all the details regarding the firewall.

* Must include specific information on package analysis tools.

It should possess strong analytical and problem-solving skills.

Certificates:

* Security +

* CCNA

* ENSA

* CISSP

* CISM

Job experience:

It is expected that you be able to graduate from Computer sciences as well as Computer engineering.

* You should possess at least 1-2 years in IT experience.

* You must have been the IT Security manager for at least one year.

* You must have prior experience with security technology as well as Processing formats (IDS / IDS, penetration tests, etc.).

Salary Variation:

Based on the research carried out in the USA In the studies conducted in the United States, it was found that the annual income is totaling $ 101,000.

Information Security Architect

Job description:

* Researches, plans, and develops strong security architectures.

* It establishes security requirements for local networks.

* Firewall, VPN, router etc. Approves and displays their configuration.

* It offers technical assistance on behalf of the security personnel.

Business Titles:

* Information Security Architect

* Information Systems Security Architect

* Cyber Security Architect

The Skills that are required:

* Should have all the information on operating systems.

* They must be well-versed in security techniques along with processing protocols (IDS or Penetration tests, IPS and so on.).

Apply IT-related strategies to the enterprise architecture and security architecture.

Certificates:

* CISSP

* CISSP-ISSAP

* CISM

* CEH

* CSSA

* GIAC certifications (GSEC, GCIH, and GCIA)

Job experience:

* It is recommended to be able to graduate from Computer Science, Computer Engineering and Computer Engineering, with a preference for.

* You must have at least 7 years of work experience working in IT as well as IT Risk Management.

* You must have at least 5 years of experience working in architectural solutions.

* Must have team-leadership previous experience.

Salary Variation:

* In the research conducted in the USA it was established that the annual earnings are $120,000 per year.

• Information Security Manager

Job description:

It creates and oversees strategies for the institution's security plan.

* It determines, implements and oversees the execution of the security policies of the institution.

It also distributes methods such as auditing, and forensics.

Business Titles:

* Information Systems Security Manager

The Information Security manager

* System Security Manager

* App Security Manager

The Skills that are required:

* He must be knowledgeable of ISO 2700/27002, ITIL and COBIT frameworks.

* Be familiar with TCP /IP and computer networks, as well as switch and routing.

* You should have good writing and verbal communication skills.

• Be aware of risk assessment techniques.

Certificates:

* CISM

* CISSP

* CISSP-ISSAP

* GIAC GSLC

Job experience:

* It is required to be able to graduate from Computer Science, Computer Engineering preferred.

* The expectation is to possess a total of 6plus years of expertise in information assurance and security.

* It is required to have the necessary experience in security-related applications for information.

Experience with team leadership is required.

Salary Variation:

* Based on the studies carried out in the USA the results have been established that the annual earnings are $ 105,000 per year.

* Director of Information Security

Job description:

It oversees and supervises IT Security programs.

* Increases the strength of IT Security technologies and programs.

* It confirms that the guidelines and procedures are followed and are properly handled by teams.

* It is responsible for preparing security reports for the board of directors.

Business Titles:

* Director of Information Security

* IT Security Chairman

* Chief of Security (CSO)

* CISO Acting

The Skills that are required:

* Extensive experience with ISO 27001/27002, ITIL and COBIT.

* He must be proficient in oral and written communication.

* He or she must be knowledgeable about TCP or IP Computer networks including routing and switching DNS, VPN.

Certificates:

* CISA

* CISM

* CISSP

* CISSP-ISSAP

Job experience:

* Ideally, it is expected that you be a graduate of Computer Sciences, Computer engineering and even hold a master's level degree.

* Candidates must possess at least 8 years of expertise in the IT field. IT.

* You must possess at least four years of experience working in an executive post.

Salary Band:

Based on the research conducted in the USA in the USA, it was discovered that the annual earnings is $111,000 total.

IT Security Certificate Programs

Certificates are an essential aspect of your professional career when you're considering an occupation in IT Security or if you have just started working in the area. Since the certificates you obtain indicate that you've reached an aforementioned level of expertise in your area. Employers today attach importance to certifications when determining the credentials of the applicant. There are numerous certification programs available in the field that deal with IT Security. We will discuss the most important and well-known certificates in this category. For each certificate we will provide the details like the institution they come from, the cost as well as the prerequisites for each levels.

Chapter 12: Cyber Security Threat Categories

Cyber-security threats to networks Security

Security threats to networks are an increasing threat to people and companies around the globe and the threat that it creates is increasing every day. However, issues with networks might not be the result of threats from outside. Insecurely configured hosts and their associated servers could pose security threats to networks. Since they consume resources in a way that is excessive, they can behave improperly and give the impression of being subject to DDoS attack, for instance. Other than that the most efficient tools are recommended to stop situations that could pose the risk of a serious danger. We can classify threats to our network as logical threats as well as resource attacks.

Logical Attacks

Logical attacks are those which exploit vulnerabilities that already exist with weaknesses and vulnerabilities which could compromise the operation or performance. This technique is highly preferred by hackers who want to destroy the structure of networks and impact performance.

A good example of this technique is using the MS05-039 overflow vulnerability.

Another kind of attack, known as "death ping" is available as an illustration. In this attack, ICMP packets bigger than the bandwidth allotted to ICMP packets are sent which causes the entire system to be impacted.

The most efficient ways to protect yourself from attacks logical is to perform necessary updates of systems and software.

Resource Attacks

This kind of attack specifically targets the resources that are crucial for the operation, like RAM and CPU. This is accomplished by sending numerous requests and IP packets through the internet. These attacks can include common botnet as well as zombie-type attacks. The malicious attacks can comprise communication infrastructure that allows them to be successful using their remote controls along with various types of attack-initiation commands.

Examples of Network Threats' Attacks Such as Trojans, Worms DDoS attack, Social Engineering Attacks, Spoofing Sniffing.

Application Risks

Security of applications can be described as the general method to test applications' security through finding, resolving, or stopping vulnerabilities and threats. These vulnerabilities and threats comprise phishing, malware, DDoS attacks, and data breach.

Mobile Applications

With the rise of smartphones and tablets using portable devices is becoming popular. In the interest of turning the situation around and are looking to devise new strategies. Strategies should be able to include a range of actions which require attention.

Theseinclude: Bring Your Own Device (BYOD) and Mobile Device Management (MDM) from Bring Your Own Device - encompasses a wide range of functions that require extensive control and user knowledge, including Mobile Device Management.

The most significant issue with security of mobile apps is that the people and businesses who manage mobile devices aren't aware of what apps they download and download perform.

Security review of mobile applications It identifies security weaknesses and configuration errors that could result in the execution of code, access upgrade leakage of data, exporting of information, as well as other security concerns.

Web Applications

Web application security is a type of security for information that safeguards an entire web-based spectrum from security breach. This includes websites, social media sites and any software utilized.

Web services are defined as a way to integrate web-based apps using open standards, such as XML, SOAP, WSDL, UDDI. All of these platforms and communication methods that cross-platform provide a variety of options for an attack.

An example of a web service review reviews how secure the online SOAP XML generator. This permits the sending of a key as well as downloading the data generated by XML.

As with a web-based application test similar to a test for web applications, this Sense of Security services test detects vulnerabilities that are predetermined within the Web service regardless of the technology that it is applied to, and also its security on the Web server or backend database that it runs on. This review outlines threats at the particular layer of application.

Examples of threats to applications: Malware, Phishing Attacks-Phishing, DDoS Attacks, Data Leak Incidents.

Host Threats

To ensure the most effective protection against current threats, as well as new threats the host's operating system and applications must be secured to a sufficient degree. Since both scenarios are mutually complementary and pose threat models from different angles Security assessments for hosts is possible to conduct independently or as part of an penetration test.

Some of the technologies being studied are:

* Operating systems

* Database servers

* Firewalls

* Routers

* Keys

* Applications for virtualization

* Balancers of load

* Intrusion Detection Systems

* Web proxy

* Web servers

* Application servers

* Mail servers

Profils of Cyber Threat Actors

Threat actors are often described as actors with malicious intent. They represent the individual (s) accountable for the events or potential events that impact the safety of an institution or individual.

State-sponsored Threat Actors They are well-funded and frequently conduct sophisticated targeted attacks. They have motives or goals due to economic, political technological, and military motives. There are information about competition resources, user searches and other sources which can be utilized to steal information.

Organized Crime Squads: These groups are known for their willingness to execute actions that yield the highest amount of profit. They typically collect personal information like the social security number of clients and employees medical records, credit cards , and bank information, and then execute ransom-related transactions using them.

Hacktivists: These hackers typically have political objectives. Their aim is to make prominent attacks that aid in the spread of propaganda or destroy the organizations they hate. Their main goal is to help them and bring attention to the issue they perceive as an issue.

People who are opportunistic They are usually amateurs and possess the desire to be noticed and well-known. But, they don't only do it for the sake of hurting. Institutions may also be able to disclose security holes discovered by the system and attempt to publish their names here. If they do they could be awarded reward points such as cash prizes, or printing names on the thank-you lists.

Unhappy Employees Dissatisfied with Their Jobs: Not all those who are involved in criminal activities against your business have to be from the outside. Employees who are unhappy with their work can join forces with other companies to earn additional income or be able to take revenge on negative circumstances in business.

Cyber Terrorists: This is that use of Internet to carry out violent acts that cause or may cause loss of life or severe bodily harm in order to make the goals of ideology or politics through intimidation or threats. They engage in actions which are considered to be as an Internet terrorist act, involving acts like deliberate, generally interrupting the computer networks of personal computers that are connected to the Internet with tools such as computer virus, computer worms and the phishing.

Spies: Cyber-spies come from individuals or groups, rivals or even governments, they attempt to acquire information in order to make the personal, economic, and military advantages to defeat the adversaries. Some examples of the actions that cyber-spies undertake is to spread malware over the Internet and network structures, or personal computers in order to get the information you want by transferring it to them.

Commercial Competitors: Businesses within the same sector may attempt to harm the opposing by causing harm to one another due to the rivalry between them. They may do this by collaborating with other individuals and institutions and also act on their own.

Motives and Goals of Cyber Security Cybersecurity Attacks

This section we'll discuss the motivations and objectives of Cyber Security attacks. In our previous article we talked about that the "Cyber Security Threat categories ".

Knowing the motivation for your enemy's actions can help you to understand how the adversaries are doing and how we can defend ourselves against them. To know what the enemy is looking for, we should be able to observe the motives behind them to force him to take this action.

Motivations to be financially motivated Threat actors might seek to make a profit in both ways. Competitors in the sector may be looking to cause harm to your company and cause financial harm in the process.

Motives from a religious perspective: You could be surrounded by enemies who wish for to ruin your reputation for your customers and reduce the quality of your service. They don't have to be threats from outside. A dissatisfied employee within the institution or an employee who had issues with the institution may have the same motives.

Political Motives: There is an increased likelihood of political motives behind state-sponsored attacks. Most attacks that are carried out at a large scale and with an enormous resource capacity are motivated by this.

Prestige and Curiosity Motive Threat actors who have they have a need to prove themselves are able to perform offensive actions in order to build a reputation and also announce their name. The motives of those who have this motivation don't have to be geared poorly. For instance, there are individuals who look for and publish their findings in institutions' systems They do this to protect themselves from huge losses , and get benefits in return.

According to the data of Radware the main goals among the acting activities of the threat actors are as follows:

* Ransom (41%)

• Internal threats (27 percent)

* Political motives (26 percent)

* Competition (26 percent)

* Cyber War (24%)

* User with limited access (20 20 percent)

* Unknown reason (11 percent)

Its primary purpose is to to make a demand for ransom with an estimated 41% cut.

Cyber-Terrorism: Intent, Capacity, Trio of Opportunities

When there is a danger To determine the danger level of a threat, the motive as well as the capacity and potential for the target need to be identified. The motive is the threat actor's intention to take action. Capacity is the ability to access resources that are sufficient to act. It is possible that there is an environment where the potential targets of an action are present and are responsive to actions.

Threatening can be considered to be integrity-based, involving the disruption of or all of the intentions, capacity or opportunity trio. From this perspective it is possible to identify threats that are legitimate when the three fundamental threat components (intent capacity, intent, and opportunity) are present as a whole. A triple threat exists as a result of fundamental dependencies. Threats could be posed if there exists at least one main component.

In an operational setting in an operational environment, the data gathered from all sources is examined for threats to discern patterns that be used to prove the attacker's motives, capacity and potential. This is evidence of the impact of the threat on the target.

Hacking Forums

Advanced Persistent Threats (APT) •
understanding advanced persistent threats

APT Terminology Definition

Advanced persistent threats (APT) are a type of hidden computer network attack in which an individual or group grants unauthorised access to a network and is not being detected for a considerable period of time. By definition, these attacks can be directly linked to nation-state-sponsored attacks, but APT can come not only from this but also from non-nation-state sources, and unauthorized access to a wide range of targets can be achieved.

APTs can serve either political or commercial purposes. APT procedures require a high level of privacy for the course of a long time.

The "advanced" method is the term used to describe complex methods which employ malware to exploit weaknesses in the system.

165

The "permanent" method means the command system continually analyzes and extracts information from a specific area.

The "threat" procedure demonstrates that the human element in the control of an attack.

The primary objective of an APT is cyber espionage, in general. Goals; the aim is to acquire sensitive data and information, such as the state of the art. Additionally, it has goals like taking funds from financial objectives as well as taking complete control of an entire system, and causing catastrophic destruction to systems and their infrastructure. Stuxnet attack is a recent attack that has caused massive sound is an illustration of APT attacks.

APT Characteristics Specifications

Targets: The final target of the threat is the enemy

Time: Time used in examining and accessing the system

sources: information, and tools resources used to reach the goal

Risk tolerance The risk's range is how far it can be without detection

Methods and Abilities Use of tools and techniques

By the threat of actions of threats and threats of

Attack Starting Points: The source points at which the action gets underway.

All the components of the attack the action is; what is the internal and external systems including components, will be affected to ensure that the grooves will be affected

Info Source: Collecting information regarding any particular threats using information gathering on the internet

Life Cycle of APT

People behind advanced persistent threats are a danger to financial assets as well as their dignity and infrastructures by following particular procedure and keeping track of the Cyber Kill Chain.

The year 2013 saw Mandiant created a cycle of life to look into attacks that were like that of Chinese APT attacks which occurred between 2004 to 2013. The life cycle includes the following steps:

Initial contact: using the 0-day virus via email using spear phishing technique and social engineering. Another method of transmission making a website which can get the attention of employees who are unhappy with their work and hiding malware.

Enhancing the connection point Installing remotely-managed malware on the victim's PC by creating access points to the internal structure and infrastructure of the computer.

Authorization upgrade: Making use of techniques for password cracking and exploits to gain access to administrative privileges on the victim's machine.

Internal discovery: Collecting information on the inner structure of the system and including the structures it's connected to, including operating system as well as the network structure.

Spread within: Expand control over other components servers, systems, networks structure, and collect information.

Make sure you are protected Steps 1 and 2 are to ensure your identity by obtaining access authorization and passwords.

Finish the task: export the data gathered through the user's networks.

Examples of APT

Sykipot APT malware family Sykipot APT family of malware exploits weaknesses within Adobe Reader and Acrobat. It was first identified in the year 2006. It's known that this malware continued to communicate with users up to 2013. The threat actors are those from the Sykipot group of malware. Government agencies have employed it in cyber-attacks against companies within and around the U.S. and the UK such as defense industries as well as telecommunications companies.

The GhostNet cyber-propagation attack was first identified in 2009. The attacks, which began in China started with the sending of emails that contained dangerous attachments. The attack has now expanded to more than 100 countries. The attackers sought at gaining access to networks of embassies and government ministries.

Stuxnet attack type of worm software developed to target the nuclear power stations of Iran. It includes four 0-days. It was discovered in the year 2010 Cyber security experts. The malware targeted SCADA (Central Audit Control and Data Acquisition) systems and spread throughout the system, thanks to an USB memory device.

APT34 APT34, a highly persistent threat group linked to Iran first came to light during 2017 by researchers from FireEye the threat group, believed to have been operating since at minimum 2014, has targeted various organizations and states across and around the Middle East.

APT37, also called Reaper, StarCruft and Group 123, is a sophisticated persistent threat organization that is a part of North Korea, which is believed to have appeared in 2012. APT37 utilized the vulnerability 0-day that was discovered inside Adobe Flash.

Chapter 13: Status Of Cissp: How To Gain And Not Lose?

Abbreviations like CISSP (Certified Information Systems Security Professional) that can be translated to "certified information security expert" began to be used in the 90s' early days, because of the association ISC2 (International Information Systems Security Certification Consortium). Nearly 90,000 people from around 146 countries already hold this title. What's the reason behind the designation of CISSP? Is it going to be recognized in the country we live in? How can I get ready for the exam?

The CISSP certification is obtained by a certified professional who has successfully passed an exam to become certified exam in addition to having the knowledge and experience in the field of technology for information and security.

It is a exam is a six-hour computer test that is conducted in English. In its structure, it is cases as well as questions related to the cases. The questions are related to subjects defined as part of the CISSP Common Body of Knowledge.

In accordance with CISSP ICS Information Security Specialists should have experience and knowledge in the following areas:

* Access control

* Network security and telecommunications

* Information security management and risk management

* secure software development

* Cryptography

* secure architecture development

* ensuring data security at an operational level

Business continuity, disaster recovery

* legislation, incident investigation, compliance

* Physical security

Take a moment to review the contents that is contained in CISSP ICS domains, the understanding of which is tested in the exam.

Control of access

This article focuses on the various the different types of access control as well as methods of authentication including biometrics, passwords and so on. Particular attention is paid to the fundamental concepts of information security like the concept for "least privilege" as well as the principle that of "need-to-know" as well as the concept of segregation of power.

Telecommunications and Security

This is the longest section that can be broken down into three blocks logically The fundamental concepts of building global and local networks, network security technology and network-based attacks.

In the first place, an expert in information security must be able to comprehend the concept of interconnections as well as using the OSI model, comprehend the concepts of "encapsulation" as well as "de-encapsulation" and be guided by the TCP IP model. In the section, LAN technologies were also included. the section, as well as components of networks like routers, switches and firewalls are also included.

For security-related technologies First of all those who will become CISSP status holders must be guided by technology that allow the creation of virtual private networks (VPN) that use networks address translation (NAT) as well as segmentation of networks. It is also essential to know the security features of wireless networks, as well as the security of email.

It is difficult to imagine a professional on the subject of security information who doesn't know the techniques used to organize cyber-attacks on networks for instance like:

* dictionary attacks using brute force;

* attacks on denial of service;

* spoofing attacks

* interception of traffic;

* attack "man standing in the middle";

* spamming attacks;

* social engineering;

* Phishing attacks

* Masquerade attacks

* session interception

* ARP-spoofing;

* DNS attacks.

Information Security Management. Risk management.

A CISSP specialist must be able to comprehend issues related to information security management.

In reality, in order to be able to pass the exam you must know the essential aspects that comprise information security. asset management as well as quantitative and qualitative techniques to evaluate the risk of security in information using security controls (security security measures) to limit risk, the creation and implementation of appropriate policies and procedures, employee education and security of information audits.

Cryptography

There is no way to think of information security without encryption. The future CISSPs do not have to possess a thorough understanding of the mathematical theories that underlie the encryption algorithms. However, they must be knowledgeable about the basics as well as the name of algorithms as well as their function. The domain covers Asymmetric and symmetric encryption methods, encryption hashing algorithm Digital Signature algorithms as well as the public keys infrastructure (PKI). Furthermore, other methods of hiding information (for instance Steganography, for example) are also considered.

Software Development Security

The majority of security issues result from software weaknesses Therefore the development of secure software field is covered by CISSP and ICS. An expert in the field of information security needs to be aware of issues such as the life cycle of software development (SDLC) as well as development and testing models as well as threats, vulnerabilities, and security measures within applications.

Security architecture

The domain covers such essential questions as the basic concepts for security model, the models for access control subsystems Security guidelines and standards, and the fundamentals of countermeasures.

Operation Security

This domain focuses on issues related to the management of operational aspects of security. This includes protection from viruses as well as patch as well as vulnerability management backup of data and recovery Compliance with the law, and information security monitoring.

Businesses Continuity and Disaster Recovery

A specialist in the area of information security must be proficient in the maintenance of business continuity as well as disaster recovery as well as evaluating the effects of disruptions on business (BIA) and testing plans and training staff.

Conformity with legal requirements

Conformity with the law is a key element in protecting information security. Particularly, security experts should be proficient regarding the requirements of law in relation to the following areas of investigations into computer criminals, protecting intellectual property rights, and licensing.

Physical security

Without the proper physically secure, security of information will be impossible. Therefore, the any future CISSP status holders must be knowledgeable about physical security threats, perimeter security concerns and server rooms.

Exam format

The exam is comprised of 250 questions that last for about two hours. Each question has four possible answers, and only one of them is right. The maximum amount of points that you can earn is 1000. In order to successfully pass the exam you need to get at least 700 points.

For example, take you can take the following variation of the question is from the CISSP candidate information bulletin:

The following description are appropriate for detecting the signs of a SYN flooding attack?

(A) Fast Internet Relay Chat (IRC) messaging

(B) creating a huge amount of semi-open connection

(C) Disabling DNS server.

(D) Linking excessively between account users and files

Correct answer Answer: B

Experience is required

The CISSP status candidate has to have five years ' experience working in at minimum two of these areas. Additionally the experience of one year may be considered in the event that the candidate holds an academic degree in security information.

Confession

Concerning what is considered to be the status of recognition it is the case in United States this status is officially acknowledged by a department such as it is the Department of Defense. For instance, in Russia the information security professional can be "required" to possess an CISSP certificate in order to be a leader on the subject of security, or be employed by an integration or consulting firm. To be able to evaluate the significance of this designation I would suggest to go through the websites of CISSPs. Social networks are a great place to start and ensure that within such professional company, it's a privilege to be a CISSP.

What is required in order to successfully pass the exam effectively?

In the view of this writer, what is most essential requirement for passing the exam is the ability to comprehend the technical aspects of English that is able to be read with using a dictionary. In the event that you are already proficient in some basic proficiency in English, it is recommended to begin your learning by mastering English terms that are relevant to the area of information security. A comprehensive glossary selection have been created and made available online on the Internet by ISACA.

To plan effectively your learning, it's recommended to begin by practicing on the various questions that are that are available via the Internet. The only thing be aware of is that you'll almost never be asked exactly the same questions on the exam because all candidates who pass are required to divulge the exam documents (and the exam number does not permit this). The practice of answering questions can help determine your weak points that require the most focus. In terms of the preparation time it is recommended to commit the minimum of three months of it. To be successful in passing an exam like the CISSP exam in the manner of a student doing the nightly task of cramming or writing cheatsheets will not do the trick. The amount of information too vast and cheating is also brutally blocked by exam organizers.

Although your experience with questions has demonstrated that your knowledge is high, it's crucial to fully comprehend the subject matter of the management of information security. Although some CISSP domains are solely technological, IS management issues increasingly dominate the exam. It's better

to cooperate with such principal resources for information security best practices such as to work with such primary sources of information security practices as ISO 27000 series standards (in particular ISO 27001 and ISO 27002) and relevant documents by NIST. American Institute of Standards (NIST).

The courses that are specifically designed allow students preparation for your exam however it is worth being aware that no single course can "load" the expertise and experience professionals have accumulated over time to an expert. The most effective way to prepare for your classes is a one-hour delivered seminar, which provides an overview of a specific area and covers some of the more "insidious" concepts, as well as examples of questions. Webinar technology today lets you participate in these classes remotely and at a convenient evening time.

We all know that it's much more enjoyable to work with someone else and, here along with engaging with your classmates via webinars, it's best to join regular forums where the future CISSP status holders debate questions to help prepare to take the exam and exchange thoughts after successful completion of the exam.

In addition, you must purchase a quality textbook. You can choose to use the official guidance of ISC2 as well as textbooks written by professional experts. Therefore, having a solid English and a thorough comprehension of IS management issues, preparation seminars, and an explanation of the textbook can help you make preparations for the exam.

Conclusion

You've completed all eight domains of the CISSP CBK. I hope that you've found useful and interesting material useful guidance, tools, and resourcesand tools to enhance your understanding and competence. I also recommend that you take advantage of all resources available to improve your the knowledge. This book is designed to prepare you to acquire the required knowledge for CISSP CBK efficiently. At the end of the day you'll be capable of applying the knowledge you have acquired in your everyday activities as a professional and prepare yourself to take the test.

If you're going to take the exam then you need a strategy. For starters, make sure you register minimum two months in advance and, during the timeframe and make use of your free time whenever you can, and do as much that you are able to.

There are a variety of CISSP study groups are available on the web. Today, there are a variety of WhatsApp groups are available to join, learn more about the subject and seek answers to your questions. Additionally, there are other books, videos and guides Security blogs Groups on Facebook, exam simulations, past-papers and many more sources you can use to get through your tests. Workshops and seminars can be a great method to learn. Today, webinars are available instead of traditional seminars in which you can take part in a simple manner.

Exam simulations and exam simulations are extremely important. Because you only have a short time, it is essential to adapt your speed and thought patterns.

Before the test, enjoy the day in peace and then get a restful night's sleep. Prior to going to the exam centre, you should eat some food as the exam can take three hours or longer according to the mode you choose. Bring drinks and snacks, along with your identification card, details for registration and add emergency medications to your list. Don't bring mobile phones and any other written material that you carry with you. During the exam make sure you take adequate breaks and stay hydrated and well-nourished.

I wish you all the best of luck along your CISSP journey